THE HERMIT

KEVIN WELLS

The Hermit

The Priest Who Saved a Soul, a Marriage, and a Family

IGNATIUS PRESS   SAN FRANCISCO

Cover design by Paweł Cetlinski

© 2024 by Ignatius Press, San Francisco
All rights reserved
ISBN 978-1-62164-700-3 (PB)
ISBN 978-1-64229-311-1 (eBook)
Library of Congress Control Number 2024936173
Printed in the United States of America ∞

He hurls down hailstones like crumbs.
The waters are frozen at his touch;
He sends forth his word and it melts them:
At the breath of his mouth the waters flow.

Psalm 147

This book is dedicated to the priests, missionaries,
and hermits who, in persona Christi,
pour themselves out.

CONTENTS

FOREWORD

by Janet E. Smith

"Jesus wept" (Jn 11:35). Why? Among all the possible reasons, including the impending destruction of Jerusalem and the pain that would involve for all the Israelites, one of the foremost surely must have been His people's hardness of heart.

There is no sorrow like unto his sorrow (cf. Lam 1:12). What was his sorrow? Not primarily the physical pain and mockery he endured, but the sinfulness of His people, especially their resistance to the graces He offers, if only they would believe in Him.

God is all-powerful, yet He allows His people to break His heart. He will not force us to love Him. He is the faithful spouse to his unfaithful bride.

Isn't it the most painful suffering of all to watch those we love self-destruct, knowing that little we say or do can move their wayward hearts? Their free will and their free choices stand in the way of their happiness and can have tremendously deleterious effects on others. You are willing to pour yourself out for your loved one, to pray and sacrifice, to listen and cajole, to remain silent, but all to no avail. Novena after novena and no results.

This story could be told by many of us. In this personal memoir of a wife's struggle with and victory over long-held shame and secret drinking, Kevin Wells—a superb

raconteur, a writer of exquisitely beautiful prose, a deeply
spiritual man, an unconditional lover of his wife, and a
man who has experienced and understands the unbeliev-
able powers of faithful priests—gives us an example of how
such a dark story can lead to a happy ending.

For my part, I would have titled this book *The Husband
and the Hermit* or *The Husband, the Hermit, and a Wife's
Recovery*. The actions of Kevin were central to the recovery of his wife, and the graces he earned through his sacrifices were vital to many of the events that providentially
occurred. It is impossible to imagine that his wife Krista's
recovery could have happened without the husband or the
hermit. Indeed, Kevin has told me that when writing this
book, he was surprised how long it took him to arrive at
the crucial interventions of Father Martin Flum, the hermit. He did not at all intend to focus on his own efforts,
but from my point of view, the Holy Spirit clearly guided
him to include this detailed account of his struggles and
strategies for helping Krista. This narrative doesn't at all
diminish the contributions of Father Flum, a holy and out-
standing priest.

It is fascinating and lovely that Kevin does not detail
what led his beloved wife Krista to seek consolation in
wine and to resist all efforts to help her. He respects her
privacy and the privacy of others whose actions wounded
her. It is extremely admirable that Krista insisted that this
story be told, clearly for the benefit of others. Indeed,
Kevin doesn't want the focus to be on Krista, or him, but
on the power of priests who truly believe—priests who
make the sacrifices and offer the spiritual guidance needed
to heal the wounded.

The story largely takes place during the COVID lockdown, when the leaders of the Catholic Church did the
unthinkable: denied access to the sacraments when they

were most crucially needed. To the great relief of the laity, a few priests found ways to work around the restrictions. Kevin and Krista are among those who blessedly had access to the sacraments and consequently experienced miraculous healings in their lives. Father Flum realized that although he could not offer the sacraments to all in his flock, he could pray and sacrifice for them, and he could offer them the opportunity for the healing graces available through Eucharistic Adoration.

Kevin has had a remarkable amount of suffering in his life. The struggle to help his wife escape from her secret drinking is just one of the trials he has faced. He and Krista first bore the cross of infertility and had to work through disagreement on what measures to take to overcome it, which included sad experiences with adoption scams. Kevin's uncle was Monsignor Thomas Wells, to whom Kevin had been closely attached from childhood. Monsignor Wells—Uncle Tommy, as Kevin had always called him—was an exemplary priest who, because of his talent for helping to save families, ailing souls, and failing parishes, had been moved from parish to parish and thus knew thousands of people. His beautiful priesthood ended early when he was reforming a parish that had been occupied for many years by active homosexual priests. Late one night, a man under the influence of drugs and alcohol showed up at Uncle Tommy's rectory, perhaps seeking a sexual encounter. It remains a mystery. Kevin's uncle was brutally murdered, an event that devastated Kevin and, in a sense, redirected his entire life. It led him to concentrate on telling stories that show how spectacular and faithful men can live out their priesthoods, while hoping to inspire priests to aim for radical holiness.

Later, Kevin faced imminent death from a horrifically painful brain bleed. He experienced a miraculous healing after a close priest friend of Father Tommy had prayed for his intercession and had a "visitation" from him. Kevin's full recovery was painful and long and coincided with his gradual realization that Krista had a drinking problem that took root in the aftermath of Kevin's close call. Because of his experiences, Kevin began wanting to live a more radically spiritual life, but Krista was not prepared to join him. A chasm opened between them. The book is a tale of the many, many sufferings Kevin and Krista endured on their journey. Currently Kevin is struggling with a knee badly mangled from sports injuries and medical disasters.

So much of the book is about Kevin, at the urging of Father Flum, digging deeply into his love for Krista and being willing to do whatever it took to rescue her. He deepened his spiritual life with more adoration, more prayer, more rosaries, more sacrifices. Nonetheless, the distance between him and Krista came to seem irreparable. He increasingly worried about how the children would be affected by the breakdown of the marriage and Krista's erratic behavior. Satan seemed to have won.

Work with various counselors promised some help but inevitably Krista returned to drinking. Kevin's inability to change Krista led him to endless prayerful introspection about his own behavior and commitments that helped him see that there were many ways that he needed to become a better person, a better Christian.

This book catalogues the steps Kevin took in this journey, the books by and about saints that he read, the constant attacks he endured as Satan tried to deter him from his efforts. Kevin does not speak in generalities or abstract terms; he offers powerful images about the details of his life, giving the reader a concrete sense of the long, hard struggle of those who know that God alone can help them and that He works on his own schedule. Kevin needed to build trust in the Lord and found his greatest challenge was maintaining hope.

Father Flum, after disappearing from the narrative early in the book, remerges about half way when Krista goes to confession to him, not realizing she had rudely slammed a door in his face several months earlier. We also learn of two other priests who helped Krista, Father Dan Leary and Monsignor John Esseff, who both had extraordinary gifts, likely bestowed upon them because of their radical commitment to their priesthood. They stepped in at crucial times to pray for and with Kevin and Krista. Kevin sketches with great precision the effect that these sensitive priests had on Krista, a sensitivity that enabled them to be brutally honest on occasion. The focus, though, ultimately shifts from Kevin and his efforts for Krista (which don't stop) to the book's keystone: the remarkable pastoral care Father Flum gives Krista, Kevin, and his whole flock.

As mentioned before, Father Flum continued to offer the sacraments throughout COVID. Remarkably, he saw the pandemic not as a curse but as a blessing, as an opportunity to cling to Jesus more closely. His approach to the lockdown, insisting upon trust in the Lord and hope for the future, dovetailed perfectly with the needs of Kevin and Krista. He made his church commit to providing thirteen hours of Adoration a day. In the end, it was much prayer in Adoration that freed Krista from her addiction.

This book is a rapid read that can often feel like a rollercoaster ride; here, I have not even sketched the bare bones. The story is truly gripping, as we see Kevin recommit himself time and again to making the sacrifices needed to help Krista, to engaging in the spiritual practices that will help him grow in his faith, and to trying to remain sincerely hopeful that Krista would beat her addiction. Krista's eventual willingness to spend hours in contemplative prayer introduces rays of sunshine into a text that yearns for the light to break through. And the catalyst and divine instrument for the long, painful healing that took place turned out to be the sacrifices, availability, and attentiveness of priests who embraced the Cross—and who teach us to do so as well.

If any readers have loved ones who are on a path to destruction yet reject all help offered to them, they will find great consolation and inspiration in this book. While patient, trusting, hopeful waiting is required, we learn that such waiting does not reduce us to being passive bystanders but requires that we offer up both involuntary sufferings and intentional mortifications. We must learn to love being with the Lord in Adoration, where we can experience His love and receive His guidance.

PROLOGUE

This is not the book I expected to write. I'd set out to tell the tale of one man: a simple priest sent by God to rescue the hurt soul of Krista Wells, my wife. Yet as this story unfurled on the screen, letter by letter, the life I saw laid bare was my own. True to his calling, the hermit faded into the background even in his own biography. "The kingdom of heaven," Jesus teaches, "is like leaven which a woman took and hid in three measures of meal, till it was all leavened" (Mt 13:33). To see the leaven, one must see the bread it raises up. To see the hermit, one must see the family that he, with the sword of Christ, saved. The story of a pastor is only as good as the story of the flock he loves. And this is just how Father Martin Flum would want it. "He must increase, but I must decrease" (Jn 3:30). With microscopic detail, the book you hold shows the action of the yeast of the kingdom, breathing new life into a marriage and life gone limp. It shows the power of what one holy priest can do when he lives out the burden of his identity and is faithful to his call until the very end, when he disappears past the bend of a country road, never to be seen again.

I imagine I am one of a pillbox-sized minority of people actually grateful for the pandemic; in retrospect, I shudder to think where my family would be without it. When forsythia was blooming into its glory in Maryland's countryside in March of 2020, and an unfamiliar strangeness covered the earth, my wife began her crawl from a tomb.

Until that saving Lenten season, everything had become neatly aligned for Krista to slide into self-devouring destruction, when fear greeted me on mornings like sirens warning of World War I chlorine gas.

Countless millions of Americans, it seemed, considered the shutdown measures that lawmakers, medical personnel, Anthony Fauci, et al., installed to be prudent and proper mechanisms for "keeping people safe" during the early stages of the pandemic. But I knew straightaway their approaches could serve as chisels to write my wife's epitaph—just as they would for countless others trapped by addictions, wounded-ness, demons, and old ghosts rising from their pasts.

It was Rome's cathedral lights that first blinked out that year, signaling the amputation of the global laity from the Holy Sacrifice of the Mass, where churches were locked and the soft glow from racks of votive candles darkened. As public Masses seemed to vanish overnight, numberless faithful Catholics wondered why bishops so quickly fell in step with the world. Overnight, the priesthood seemed to have become expendable, a "nonessential" part of life, as many were restrained from going to hospitals and into the hearth fire of homes to calm the frightened and confused souls now even more desperately in need of Christ's heal-ing presence. Riding a bicycle to the moon was easier than finding an unlocked chapel.

Meanwhile, the neon-lit signs of twenty-four-hour casinos, liquor stores, and reduced-capacity strip clubs blinked on after sundown like strings of multicolored Christmas lights for gamblers, alcoholics, and voyeurs. Murders proceeded at a normal clip at Planned Parent-hood facilities, and the brokenhearted elderly wept alone in companion-starved, tang-smelling hospices, their de-sertion like a biblical plague. Many of them took their last breath in their rooms alone, abandoned, unloved, and barred from a priest's anointing. Many families were forever scarred by the denial of an opportunity for a last goodbye or to make amends before their loved ones passed on. A white flag waved to the enemy of souls in those final moments when the devil seeks most to wrest souls from the bosom of the Most Sacred Heart, when previously, it was the priest who stood in the way as defender of the dying. Sacramental burials suddenly became denied until it was deemed "safe" to lower down the dead properly and with prudence.

May God have mercy on us for our behavior during this time. To many, the thin edifice of human reason and compassion seemed to melt like wax in the face of a virus that was real and certainly took the lives of many, but that for the general public was nowhere near the Moby-Dick-sized man-eating killer it was portrayed to be. Regardless of the reality of the threat, within a few weeks of COVID's global spread, political, medical, and Church leaders collaborated to harpoon and seamlessly bring down a worldwide economy and simultaneously bar Catholic churches and other houses of worship throughout the world.

Through a seeming lack of imaginativeness in creating cautious ways to feed their flocks during the time of pandemic, bishops took away the Flesh of Christ—the lifeblood and source and summit of our faith (see paragraph 1324 of the *Catechism*). The Great Disruptor had seamlessly managed to weave itself into the most sacred fabrics of the Church in the manner Jesus explained as the knitting together of the wheat and tares.

Certainly, my emotions about what I saw as the Church's betrayal and abandonment were stoked by my desolation. I had been in the midst of a long dark night, where for the first time in my life, my trust in God was flickering in and out.

As the global crop-dusting of fear pressed down, my wife was secretly drinking most nights. She had been for years. When the universal machinery megaphoned "*isolate*," I couldn't imagine a more dooming word for my family. I will never forget the bark— "*isolate!*"—that barreled into the world like Gadarene swine to stoke further the isolation and self-preservation that seemed to have redefined humanity. The lamentable word was a harbinger of the winter storm I knew was coming to my home.

For years, it was isolation and secret places that offered Krista endless acres of opportunity to speed up her demise. Much of her previous several years were spent in what seemed a garden of neatly aligned rows of hidden red wine bottles. When the COVID-19 clock struck, I had premonitions that the secret garden would expand, where wounds and dark habits would bloom and produce summering fields of stench.

Then, something happened.

When virtually all Catholic priests were mandated by bishops to shutter their doors for the sacrifice of the Mass and all of the other sacraments, one priest searched the words of God, carved like stained glass windows into his soul, and kept his open.

It was a dark bargain Father Martin Flum (rhymes with *bloom*) made in order to celebrate private Masses with the back door of his church unlocked. But instinctively he understood that the duty of his sacred state demanded he take risks for the laity he loved; he had been ordained to search beyond the natural order to see what lay beneath and beyond edicts and warning words. He was the slaughtered lamb *in persona Christi*, a father of souls of earth, not a hypervigilant restrainer of God's graces. In that vein, he also knew the Holy Sacrifice of the Mass—though experienced *in* the world—was not *of* the world; its sacred purpose was invincible, and its spiritual effects far transcended the physical effects of a virus. The Lamb will always be stronger than a dragon, no matter its form and dimension.

Before the ink was dry on lockdown orders that Father Flum understood would deny many the very specific forms of sanctifying grace they needed—escalating their remoteness from God—he had begun to descend the spiral staircase into Krista's shame. It was there where he as the Good Shepherd began to pull from her soul, one by one, defects and habits that for so long had seemed to me to be untamed beasts.

It wasn't just my wife, though, that he came for. As a growing crescendo of priests began to isolate from their flock, Father Flum began to lavish fatherly care on whoever was willing and within his reach in the backcountry town of Baden, Maryland, where acres of farmland and faded wooden tobacco barns mark memories of the town's old cash crop.

In this modern-day telling of a *Diary of a Country Priest*, perhaps some pastoral allegory can be excused here to set a tone. When the dark accoutrements of the pandemic first began to fall, Father Flum emerged as a cassocked farmer in dawn's purple twilight; a quiet watcher leaning up against a porch post surveying his suddenly winter-dead fields. After a long time of stroking the whiskers of his Old Testament beard, he grinned the grin of one who knows and stepped into his pasture. He began to rip scarecrows from his fields and go about the spiritual work of turning over, tilling, and trellising souls—the souls of *his* pasture—so that, when the pandemic lifted, the harvest would still be gathered. He personally chased away all the wild-eyed crows and daily scattered the circling vultures that encroached upon the unmarked boundaries of his Saint Michael's parish grounds. He built immovable barricades with scattered holy water and blessed salt that became like rings of iron around every square inch of the perimeter of his spacious parish grounds. With a blood loyalty to his purpose and duty, he cleared out the copperheads, mice, cutworms, earwigs, and moles from fields made barren by an infestation of mandated isolation, sacramental moratoriums, and spiritual neglect. Then he scattered the seeds of God.

This image of a spiritual farmer sowing seeds of hope might well be lost on the countless millions who have lost sight of the supernatural reality of a transcendent God, those who find laughable the invisible plains covered with long-lanced angels and the charred souls of demons at war. But those who *see* the supernatural might bow their head in deference to the extent of the measures Father Flum took each day in the service of souls between 2020 and 2021, when he courteously opened his heart to every appeal that came his way. He took a different line to the Great Disruptor. With the consistency of the cockcrow, he fought against it through the steely-edged textiles of sustained fasts, bodily and emotional mortifications, self-denials, devotions, processions, and warmhearted contemplation of his Queen, the Mother of God. He took risks to guard his flock.

Each evening at 9:00 P.M., for most of 2020, he stood behind Saint Michael's ambo, where he seemed to be spiritually transmogrified while imploring Saint Michael the Archangel and the Heavenly court to protect his parishioners. Because he knew the spread of demons had been given a wide berth through the sacramental famine instituted by the pandemic, he shielded his parish through the long exorcism prayers used during special circumstances. Even-toned and deliberate in speech, his tone dramatically changed during those nightly prayers, where the pitch of his voice rose and fell like a wild sea.

One rebellious spirit, though, got in—at least that's what some folks from this neck of the woods have come to believe. Beneath a summer moon one night, Father Flum was slammed into his parish's hard asphalt parking lot. When he walked into the sacristy for Mass the next day, face badly bruised and dragging a leg, few dared to ask what had happened. To one man, though—one of his closest friends—Father Flum spoke a few words about it. In no more than a sentence or two, the man became frozen.

COVID-19 in Baden, Maryland, was a wondrous time. Marriages were healed by the fiercely bearded priest. A young man discerned his call to the seminary. A suffering young lady began to spend time with an order of nuns and discern religious life. A family was brought into the Church. A man whose heart failed was given a second chance. "The Wings," a group of young adults, found a priest with a bigness of heart like John Bosco, who warmed them with the storytelling of the saints and by joining them for softball games.

A blessed group of fortunate Catholics paid witness to the inner life of this shepherd's old soul during a period of fear, seeming fanaticism, and spiritual fatherlessness. Those who acted as fathers during this time know who they are: as do those who mostly absconded. Many clergy members shepherded their flocks with magnanimity and ardor throughout the pandemic, but I am not certain if a single priest could have done it as completely and counter-vailingly as Father Flum, who helped a small town flower when the world seemed to wither.

Krista has asked me to open the curtains on one simple priest whom God thrust into her life to save her. In the aftermath of her healing, she wanted to cast a floodlight on the potency of a pastor who ceded no ground in lift-ing her to God when few shepherds could be found. At a time when laity searched high and low for lionhearted witnesses like Damien the Leper, Joan of Arc, a plague hero the likes of Charles Borromeo or John Bosco, they instead watched in defeat as priests abandoned their quest and settled peaceably behind rectory doors, ramping up the celebration of video Masses and parish Zoom meetings. Krista and I paid witness to the opposite behavior in Father Flum, who ran contrary to those bishops who in their haste toward caution—in considering the mortal body over the immortal soul—contributed to something apocalyptic: millions of Catholics left the Church.

It is certain that many faithful and good priests suffered fitful nights of sleep, or even awakened from nightmares where the vow of obedience, canon law, and higher orders helped strangulate their desire to live their priesthood magnanimously. Perhaps the old Catholic grit of bold shepherding has reached its nadir, and a second or third globally pervasive moratorium of the sacraments and Masses and locked churches is inevitable. One wonders, though, how dutiful priests might adjust their behavior should future shutdowns be issued by their bishops.

This tale, though, is of the life-changing reality of a priest who refused to shut down—and the imperishable gift he became to my wife and me when a pope, his bishop, and so many fellow priests conformed to protocol and caution and, with a few exceptions, seemed to fade away. This is a story of our lives and the closing chapter for us of what many believe and experienced to be pastoral masterwork. Perhaps it will inspire a reawakening for holy priests down the millennia.

Perhaps it will even provide what some might see as a blueprint for future days (others will surely find it scandalous) on the manner in which a priest must act to both guard and nourish souls at a time of widespread chaos—without ever considering ramifications, the response of the world, or even the response of Church hierarchy. In this strange new era of global health consciousness, some will flinch at the idea of a priest not considering how he might jeopardize his own, or another's, physical health during COVID, but Father Flum didn't. Throughout the pandemic, he considered only how he stood with God and his calling to save souls.

How he stood was revealed mostly in the shadow of candlelight, at the base of a golden monstrance, where he disappeared for many hours each day. Day after day, for the entirety of the pandemic, he placed himself as a beggar before Jesus at Adoration, where he pleaded for divine prudence, greater wisdom, a stiffening of his resolve, and the best practical ways to shepherd his parish toward peace and grace.

What follows shines a light on the unspoken action of a holy priest who shepherded souls during a pandemic. As for Krista, this story perhaps goes deeper, in revealing the manner in which a priest finally teased out weariness, dark habits, and hardened lies ... and peeled back scabs of cynicism to allow space for her finally to see the face of God. I thank God each day for Father Flum—for Krista had become unreachable to me. In her pain, she had lost sight of the supernatural value of her God-touched soul; so, Father Flum stepped in to explain why it mattered and how it was a timeless masterpiece.

He will never be seen again. Father Flum has crossed over the shores to another place, to what Homer called the *winedark sea*, where he has gone off to face the demons alone in the far countryside of solitude. He has buried himself in the ocean-wide depths of God's heart as a consecrated hermit.

His home today is a cell, likely no larger than your childhood bedroom, buried deep in a forest, hidden among tens of thousands of trees. There, he offers the remainder of his life to beg God's mercy on a broken generation. *He is a holocaust offering for us, a living human shield who has forfeited every comfort for renewal in the priesthood.* As you read this sentence, he is almost certainly praying. And if you are a hardy and believing soul who takes the might of sacrifice seriously, you might feel inclined to fall to your knees in joy and thanksgiving for a life that brims over with visceral love for God. Because you know he has also disappeared to save *you*, to become a one-man army for *you*, as he wages spiritual war against the rising tide of disorder in the Church and world.

One evening, in the dead of winter 2021, six months after Father Flum steered his high-mileage silver Toyota truck from his sleepy parish for the last time, Krista proposed a remarkable idea. She asked me to write the story of her once-sick soul and how Father Flum worked to purify it. Shy by nature, Krista told me she felt God had called her to expose herself so that the priesthood of Father Flum could be exposed. She wanted me to shine a bright light on her broken years—*our broken years*—and what a cassocked repairman did to piece her back together.

No was my answer.

As months passed, Krista occasionally asked me to reconsider. One day, I told her I would spend time in prayer about it. When, after a few more months, she told me that "my praying was delaying," I told her I would try. So, with her blessing hand, I sat at my desk like a stone. When she asked how the writing was going, I told her my fingers kept dangling over the keyboard like bothered cobras, not knowing where or how to strike. *How does a husband press down on a letter key to begin a sentence detailing the chaos of the one he loves and its effects on him and his family?*

"God might not want your story revealed," I said. "Especially by your husband."

"That's where you're wrong," she said. "This story is about a priest who showed no fear. Show people what he did to save my life during the pandemic—how a *man* behaves. Now, write."

Chapter 1

The Visit

The moon was rising above our frozen field when Krista opened our front door no wider than the width of a Webster's Dictionary. Cold winter air pushed into our stone-flagged foyer. It was dinnertime on February 8, 2016, when my thirteen-year-old son, Sean, told his mom that a man had been knocking on our door. She had heard the knocking, but ignored it. Behind the locked door of our bedroom, Krista had been drinking.

She put the wine bottle away, tucking it inside her black leather equestrian boot in the corner of our closet. Then, walking through the hallway to the front door, she set herself to dismiss quickly the Seventh Day Adventist, salesman, neighbor, or whoever the nuisance was at this moment.

I often picture the night Father Flum looked into Krista's eyes for the first time. Once, he shared with me that sorrow wrung his heart that night.

This is how Krista remembers that night.

The porch was unlit. Beneath the moonglow was the silhouette of a slender man with a stunning beard; it was as broad and messy as Karl Marx's, an imperial nest of white and gray of biblical bearing that spread to the top button of his black wool jacket. The night was graveyard silent. The stranger was of average height and had graying hair shaved close to his head. He stood in the stillness looking directly at Krista through the three-inch door crack. He kept his hands buried in his coat pockets. "He looks like a roadside hitchhiker," was my wife's first mental image and consideration of the man.

She squinted into the lengthening shadows and studied his manner more deeply. She saw that beneath his coat was a black cassock with a thin vertical alignment of a few dozen small buttons stretching from his collar down to the tops of his shoes. She recognized that it was a Catholic priest standing before her. He resembled an over-embellished character from an earlier period, like the long-nosed, tight-ponytailed Ichabod Crane.

Then, suddenly, fear ran through her body like poison. *He knows me and what I am doing.* Unbeknownst to her, Father Flum had spent the day fasting for this visit.

Getting hold of her emotions, Krista stared into the priest's dark brown eyes and recognized an intelligence and depth. Behind his unfashionable glasses were kind, warm eyes. She saw that swallowed up within his venerable beard was what seemed the smile of a humble man from the countryside. She perceived in his essence a well of benevolence. A man of strength and peace stood before her in the moon's shadows. Perhaps due to her secret shame and his seeming authority, she flinched, broke eye contact, and lowered her eyes upon his Old Testament beard.

When Father Flum saw the disharmony lodged in Krista's ringed eyes, a movement of sorrow pierced him. Standing before him was what seemed like a self-destructing soul. He noted her inability to maintain eye contact. He saw, too, that she seemed to be antagonized by his presence—or at least had an outward frustration for the net in which he knew that she had found herself caught. It was true. Krista told me later she was furious that Sean had answered the door, and even more enraged that it was a priest who stood before her as the visitor.

"Hello, there," Father Flum said softly, reassuringly. "I'm Father Flum, and I guess I'm here for dinner." Gentle puffs of wintertime vapor airlifted from his beard. He stood beneath a bare branch of the red maple that extended over our small porch.

The crack of the door remained a slit. Although the light switch was within reach, the porch stayed dark. Rather than sweetly faking a welcome smile of cordiality, she became immediately coldhearted. Her eyes became slits.

"Kevin's not here. He didn't tell me anything about a dinner tonight," Krista spat back. "I didn't know anything about you coming here. Who are you?"

"I'm sorry your husband didn't let you know. My name is Father Flum. I'm not sure what happened. You must be Krista ... I'm a friend of Kevin's. We got to know one another at the retreat in Faulkner," he explained.

"He didn't tell me anything about you," she responded, flatly. "And he didn't tell me anything about a dinner."

"Oh, well, Kevin must have gotten things mixed up. He arranged a dinner for us at your home tonight. I drove quite a way—*and I'm hungry,*" he said cheerfully from the shadows, not betraying his discomfort at the unwelcoming. "Would you mind if I stepped in? It's cold out here."

Krista inventoried his words. And from her interior came a single thought: *This night is meant for sabotage. It is a siege.* It was then that a rebellion, a dark vein of defiance, sprang from within her. Fury lay heavy in her eyes. Abruptly, she worked to gain hold of what she was certain was a plan to address her drinking. Her eyes became cold orbs as she stiffened herself to get rid of him. She no longer looked into his beard; she looked directly into his eyes.

"I know nothing about this. And I have no idea who you are," she said icily, intensely staring at him. "Why don't you call my husband and ask him why he's not here?

He's a thousand miles away from us right now. Great planner he is."

Father Flum was disarmed by her sarcasm. He fell into a bemused look, the awkward and pure smile of a kindergartner at his first picture-taking. "Well, this is a bit indelicate. How's this—I'm not a picky eater. Whatever you've got, I'll eat. I'm a hungry priest who hasn't had much of anything today." The oven was cold. The kitchen was dark.

"No. Again, I know nothing about you or this," she said, her coiled voice rising. An icy stillness held, as if she were protecting herself against something leprous.

"Well, maybe we can sort things out inside," he offered quietly. "You've been impositioned, and I apologize. I don't want to put you out with a meal, but maybe we can talk for a bit."

"No," she said loudly, with a glacial gaze.

The priest stood wordless. The inner turbulence, he saw, was enormous. Pity covered him.

"There's a Wawa on the corner up the road," Krista said, filling the silence with the tide of anger foaming in her. Then she finished him up, remarking as she closed the door. "Get something to eat over there."

From the long vertical windows on the sides of each door, Krista saw that Father Flum stood motionless for a while on the porch. After some time, he turned and walked back to his truck with a faded "MARY-land" bumper sticker. The truck remained, engine turned off, for ten or so minutes. For a while, Krista spied on him from a window in our living room, looking at the silhouette of his truck. She didn't know that he was likely commanding prayers of deliverance. Figuring he was making a phone call, she grew bored and went back into our bedroom, closed and locked the door, where she rummaged through the closet and recovered the bottle from inside the boot.

These seven years later, Krista believes that as she was getting drunk, Father Flum was scattering blessed salt and water where the frozen ground ran up against the brick veneer at the edge of our home. With her inner eye in retrospect, she sees the vapor trail from his breath that night carrying prayers of deliverance for an afflicted soul, unscented incense released into the soft winter night, carried on swirling breezes past constellations to the throne of God. The invocations most surely marked the first of what would become Father Flum's numberless prayers to wrest the stronghold of alcohol and woundedness from Krista's grip. In her imagination, my wife still sees Father Flum untangling his cassock from dead shrubbery and undergrowth as he proceeds down the border of our home like a nocturnal termite inspector. She believes now it was that winter evening when the big-bearded priest began to pull her soul from Hell.

I couldn't have known it then, but an unseeable, single strand of a gossamer thread of hope for Krista and my family spun into existence that night. A seemingly unwinnable war launched against a secret addiction that was annihilating my marriage and family. A holy priest took hold of the kingdom of darkness in my wife. Although nothing went as humanly planned that night, I imagine Father Flum traveled the moonlit country roads back to his parish with a secret smile. I believe he was as collected as a man can be when a door is slammed in his face. I also suppose he may have wondered, on a more natural level—*Where was Kevin?*

I had just finished climbing a dirt path on a hill deep inside the Jamaican interior when I felt the buzz of my phone in my pocket. I was on a short mission trip with fourteen others in womb-to-tomb communities that care for the severely developmentally and physically disabled scattered throughout the small island nation.

After traveling a winding road through green-carpeted mountains, we arrived at Jacob's Ladder, the largest of the Mustard Seed Communities built on an old bauxite mine. It was a thriving village where more than one hundred adults with disabilities were treated with compassion and care, many of whom had arrived as abandoned youngsters.

After unpacking, our group began to walk down a narrow path to small cottages dotting the valley at the bottom of a hill. I read Krista's text: *How dare you! A priest comes over without you saying a word. Great job. Way to plan it out! I didn't let him in.*

I stopped. A tremor seemed to break open in me. *Oh, man. I forgot. Oh, no.* Heavy weariness immediately overcame me, as if I had just swum up from the bottom of the sea.

It seemed a hatchet had swung into my head, splitting open a dam of discordant images of Krista. In each, a cauldron brimmed over with disgust for me. For this mistake, I would pay. Absentmindedly, I had forgotten to write down the date of the dinner appointment we had arranged months earlier. As my traveling companions carried on animated conversations walking down to the village, I stood still on the path and sweated profusely, as if liquid hatred flung from Maryland poured over me, immobilizing me.

Five hours earlier, I had been sitting on a small bench beside a frail reed of a child, who looked to be all of eight or nine years old. She had contracted the AIDS virus at birth. She lived in a tender community of abandoned children in a village carved into a mountainscape. Her home, situated several miles down a dirt road with potholes the size of elephants, looked more lonesome than Pluto. The quiet girl was beautiful sitting alone in front of a weather-beaten wooden structure that resembled a chicken shack.

In her hand was a thin notebook, one of those miniature 3″ × 5″ steno pads parents used to buy their children to write down homework assignments. Its cardboard protective covering was creased and flimsy. Only fifteen or so pages, some stained, remained within the notepad.

I asked if she wouldn't mind me writing her a note. Unsmiling, and without a word, she nodded and handed the tiny pad to me. I opened it and saw that every page except the first page was blank. A two-line letter was written to her father.

> *Daddy,*
> *I am waiting for you to come.*
> *It will be good to see you.*
> *Love,*
> [Name forgotten]

Later, I asked a caretaker how often her father visited. She told me there was no contact with Mom or Dad. There never had been and likely never would be. Burning tears began to well.

As I now worked to pull together and reorder my emotions after receiving Krista's text, emotions already vulnerable, I trudged back down the path alone, floundering in disgust at myself for my grave mistake. I knew precisely how she would interpret the visit from the unknown priest: it was my ransacking, two-against-one attempt to stop her from drinking. On this sun-splashed, encouraging day, I knew that shortly after my homecoming in Maryland, I would be entering a place of land mines.

As the day moved on, disappointment in myself and my carelessness shifted to feelings of anger for Krista. I resented marrying a woman whose sickness *compelled* her to kick a priest off our doorstep. I felt physically and emotionally drained, wearied by the strain of being married to a woman who had been secretly binge drinking for years. God, it seemed, had turned his face from me. Thousands of prayers, fasts, and Rosaries for Krista seemed to be remorselessly ignored. Desolation covered me in the jungle.

God, why? Where are you?

He was there. He was right there that morning in the face of the child with the notepad, whose scrawled words revealed the sacred blueprint. She hoped. This stunning girl hoped in absolute darkness, like a leprous girl from a forgotten island asking a far-flung God for a father, and later watching a man named Damien dock his boat. I didn't, though, have that level of hope then. I didn't see God or how He was trying to speak to me. I stopped believing in the mysterious ways of His providence—even though he had already sent a priest.

Father Flum had entered my life the previous December when a retreat director invited him to present a talk on the Holy Trinity. As he made his way into the countryside chapel on a cold winter night, he resembled a portrait of an Amish pastor peeled from a farmhouse wall. Head bowed, breviary and Bible in hand, he walked with authority past eighty or so men in his worn cassock that whooshed with each quick step he took. His unruly salt-and-pepper beard bobbed slightly as he made his way to a slender wooden lectern. A perfect serenity and benevolent haze seemed to trail him. None of the men I knew at the silent retreat had ever seen him before. He quickly scanned the faces in the chapel with what seemed magisterial assuredness, smiled slightly through his beard, and began his lecture.

The mysterious priest didn't spend a moment warming us up, explaining who he was or where he was from. He became a pure block of resolve and efficiency, but the suppleness and calm of his voice were relaxed; it seemed a tone Beloved John may have had when conversing with Mary in Ephesus. His talk didn't include a single joke, story, or non sequitur. His teaching carried authority, and each of his thoughts cohered with the next. Not a single sentence was marred by *uh*'s or *um*'s. He was masterful in expounding on the Trinity's interconnectedness—every word designed to transport us to the core of the triune God—where three heartbeats joined as one. Although the chapel was stuffed with men, and the balcony full, we sensed he was speaking more for God than to us. His grasp on the mysterious interflow of the Trinity seemed spoken directly into his ear by each of the three Persons of the Trinity themselves. It was airtight and above our intellect; we were eavesdroppers on what God had lodged deep into his soul.

Mostly lost to time are his words, but I recall that as he spoke, retreatants seemed to begin to regard the stranger as more a mystic than a priest. What he shared had been pieced together through monk-like prayer, the reading of ancient holy books, and years of Scripture. Most in the room, I imagine—definitely me—were in over our heads, but every now and then we fastened ourselves to a word, thought, or an image and found ourselves caught in the undertow of something we felt in our souls. On this bitterly cold night, the chapel for us seemed to catch a sweet fire. This uncommon priest spoke to us as if Christ had just nonchalantly whispered the words into his ear.

Later that evening, I sought him for confession. I wanted to sit across from him and confess the sin of my growing despair. As I sat, he looked with warmth into my eyes. I had been coming to this retreat house on the same December weekend since my college days, for more than a quarter of a century—and I had never before sat across from a priest resembling a desert father. I told him I was losing hope in God, and I was losing hope my wife would stop binge drinking, which she had been doing now for a growing number of years. He leaned forward in his cassock and rested his forearms on his thighs. He looked into the middle distance and remained quiet as I spoke of my despair. When I finished, he remained noiseless.

After the silence, Father Flum sat upright and looked straight into me. His eyes were grave. "It is a cross," he said, "but this cross must continue to be carried. Despair will make it impossible. Is this a cross you want to keep carrying for your wife?"

"Yes, Father," I said. "Of course I do ... I sort of have to." He smiled.

He edged me closer to understanding the sweet violence of carrying a cross for one who has become an island unto herself. He said spouses must climb dark mountains for their beloved, explaining the discouraged spouse was obliged to shoulder the cross as a gift of patient love for the tormented spouse. He asked if I were fasting, then urged me to commit to many more sacrifices and self-denials for Krista. If I surrendered my wife completely to God and trusted fully in His paternal love, he said, God would begin to bring light and heal her wounds.

"It is time," he said softly, "for you to practice patience as you hand her over to God. Patience, especially in a situation as difficult as this one, is very hard, but you must be patient now as God continues His reparative work in Krista.

"In time, this will end. The Father knows her agony and yours, and he knows your concern for your children, but He has absolute power to remove this darkness. Your wife is very troubled, and He has the power to take it all away."

He continued, warning me. "But again, you must fully trust God. You cannot fix this. In time, God will. Your spouse will heal if you hand her over to Him completely. Accompany Him on this journey by giving her your love and continued prayers and fasting."

After confession, I prayed in silence in the now-darkened chapel, considering the tenderness and weight of Father Flum's words. His straightforward words were the lone option. It was an absolute surrender of Krista and patient resignation I needed to give God. At the same time, I knew with certainty that night, fully activating this type of surrender would mean traversing a rocky road that would only worsen until I mined my depths and grabbed my soul as if it were a facemask and reoriented it back to trust in God.

I begged the Holy Spirit to give me the wisdom to love Krista well when I returned home. Although her secret drinking had taken on a frightening permanence, it came to me that Satan's hostile takeover of Krista could come to an end if I worked through God alone. Krista needed an immovable man who would quietly love her, a man who would accept his role as an intimate outsider removed from her landscape studded with land mines. My burden was simply to keep watch from the other side of the wall—and to die to everything I had once hoped for—and to begin to hope again, in a different, supernatural way.

When his last penitent departed, and Father Flum stepped from the confessional, I asked if he wouldn't mind coming to our home for dinner, where I hoped he could begin to build a relationship with Krista and my family. I knew upon offering the invitation that Krista would not want an unfamiliar priest in our home, but I told myself I would deal with the fallout when the time came. Better to apologize than ask permission. He smiled and said he would appreciate that. "It would be good to meet your family," he said. "And Krista." Right then we settled on a date—the date I foolishly neglected to write down.

On this day, Krista seethed in our home as I stood on a dirt path under a suddenly bleak sky. Accompanying her anger, I knew, was her behind-closed-door consumption of red wine. Her dark custom had become an unholy life-blood. My children were none the wiser, but I knew this time would soon be ending. They were growing older, and Gabby and Sean were no dummies.

From Jamaica later that evening, we boarded an ancient half-sized bus that shimmied up winding jungle-mountain roads. Thick canopies of trees swallowed up the moon and stole every wink of starlight. If the bus' headlights had blinked out, we would have experienced the shade of darkness glimpsed only at the bottom of the sea. Our destination was a small resting place known by pilgrims and local Catholics as "Widow's Mite."

The day's events had released into my head a lava flow of tension. I also was vainly imagining Father Flum driving the hour back to his country parish, considering the fool who invited him into his home for dinner and forgot all about it. The greater portion of my thoughts, though, were on poor Krista, my three children, and the lost evening that could have been spent with this uncommon priest.

It was late when tired folks began dropping into narrow beds scattered randomly throughout a room. Because turbulence was still barreling through my head, I knew sleep would be difficult. I quietly asked the chaplain of the retreat, Father Dan Leary, if there was a place to pray in solitude. He led me in total darkness down a path to a small chapel at the rear of the building. He flicked on a light and departed to help settle folks in. I sat on a wooden pew and cast my eyes on a small Tabernacle. From the open chapel door and windows came a sustained chorus of loud insects. As a boy, I'd fall pleasantly asleep to the melody of male crickets singing, and other nocturnal bugs, but my disconsolation had turned the night symphony into a heavy rush of noise, seemingly birthed from demons. It became a cacophonous hiss: *We will ruin your time with God. We have ruined your life.* I could not pray, and the riot of noise seemed to increase in decibels concordant with the coming apart of my soul. With my bleary eyes trained on the Tabernacle, I wept. The small girl with the steno pad clung to a false sliver of hope, and on this night, I felt I had none.

After some time (I read later from my journal), my thoughts fell on my youngest daughter, Shannon—where a weight became lifted. The thought of her gentle and quiet way reminded me of the young girl with the steno. They were about the same age. From the jungle-side chapel, I imagined sitting beside her on the couch back home in Maryland, watching another episode of *Little House on the Prairie*, which had become our shared nightly custom. On the wide-open plains of Minnesota, there was order in the Ingalls' frontier home; a humble rightness to things. As Shannon became swept into another episode's story line, I frequently thought of Krista and her phantom. As Shannon watched, I often prayed, begging God to bring Krista's soul to order, where she would be content (in a silly way) like Charles, Caroline, "Half-pint," and the rest of the Ingalls family, to sit peacefully by the hearth fire, relaxing with a book and sipping from a teacup instead of a bottle of wine.

Father Leary eventually reappeared with his breviary. He knew of Krista's drinking; he was the only one, other than God and Father Flum, who understood the magnitude of the endless Passion play of destructive behavior and the pattern of her secretive drinking. I told him earlier on the trip about the isolation and what felt like a supernatural force of evil pressing down in my home.

The priest sat in silence, praying a few pews in front of me. His presence was a leaven and unspoken support, a buoy in the unruly sea of my thoughts. The bedlam of the insects in the darkness softened. And I felt a gap of calm open for me to pray. *Oh, Mary, Mother me now. Oh, Mary, my soul is empty. Mother Krista now. Mother my poor children. Protect them all from it.*

Chapter 2

The Beginning

In a secret place of my thoughts resides a memory, a metaphorical scar of an image, of what the beginning of Krista's drinking felt like.

She walks into the cold waves of the surf, slowly pulling farther from the safety of the shoreline. It is a sunny, blue-sky day. Small children chase seagulls. Teenage boys bodysurf, and moms on beach chairs read summer fiction novels with their toes in the water.

Krista is completely alone, caught in the swell of an undertow. Nobody notices her. The same scene plays out over and over: Krista is in the tides, her back turned to the beach. Her silhouette slowly vanishes. At this sitting, I am covered by consuming sadness. As I scream for her to swim in, she zombies farther out as if an invulnerable force compels her. She no longer feels the sand beneath her feet.

Bothered seagulls careen and circle, screeching just above her, the lone creatures paying her mind. As I swim through the break of waves to get to my wife, I see to my horror that she is no longer there. All around is the chop of the sea. She is gone now, I know.

The ocean becomes wilder and colder, and stygian darkness begins to cover the shoreline. The crying seagulls have now become quietly circling vultures. And the realization comes to me: *she lives beneath the sea now, in a place I cannot reach.*

I look back to the beach, beyond the break of the waves, and see that the shoreline is now deserted, save for the silhouettes of three small figures. A fog has pushed in. I make out the images of three small children. They look out, waiting for me to swim back in with their mom.

To arrive at the point of Krista's eventual reemergence requires seeing her beneath the swallowing sea. The story should be written as it was. I imagine some writers desert manuscripts because of an inability to "write through" troublesome memories, memories that expose dark, manhandling shame and reveal the places of pandemonium. For this book to serve its purpose—to reveal the startling manner of what a holy and unsparing priest did for Krista and me during the pandemic—some of those brokenhearted events need to be told. I will not dwell on or write about some of the more macabre moments—as it would be cruel and is not the aim of this book—but some dark memories do serve as a starting point.

Like a pearl diver, Father Flum swam straight down into the sea's depths, where through the darkness he saw a pinhole of light. He knew it was the glow of a soul, so he swam down in his waterlogged cassock with an expression of determination, down to the very bottom, where he gathered into his tired arms the broken flower he knew was my wife. He pushed off from the ocean floor and kicked through the black sea for the surface, cradling a mostly drowned soul.

This was the night I am conscious of it beginning, the time when my home would come to feel haunted. This was when the dark winds came and my world as I knew it would, little by little, begin to fall away.

I had returned home after a three-week stay in a Baltimore hospital, where it seems I was as close to death as one can be. Knotted blood vessels previously unknown had abruptly released in my cerebellum one night, and despite many attempts, doctors couldn't control the blood that was drowning my brain. A day after a failed invasive surgery, a Catholic priest and friend, Father Jim Stack, came to my ICU room and begged the intercession of my late uncle, Monsignor Thomas Wells, who had been murdered in his rectory in 2000. Thereafter, Father Stack said he was standing amidst something supernatural, as he watched the room become cast in warm light and a Heavenly court descend. Doctors had no explanation for the blood, fluids, and arteriovenous malformation that had vanished the next day as mysteriously and quickly as an absolved mortal sin. Fifteen years later, Father Stack's voice still trembles when retelling what happened in that room.

After a lengthy hospital recovery, I was sent back home, healed. However, because brain surgery carries venomous reverberations, I suffered. At various points during each day, it seemed like an elf with a machete swung at the matter in the center of my brain. I couldn't walk. Resting on top of my neck was a head that felt as large and heavy as a pumpkin. My handwriting was illegible. I couldn't see well. Because my cerebellum had been sliced up, if I raised my head too quickly, I would vomit.

My brush with death was over, and I was told by my surgeon that the "inconveniences" needed to be patiently endured and overcome. At home, I was lifted up the stairs into my bedroom, where I asked Krista to shut every blind and darken every lamp. Light in any form brought on headaches like large horseshoes flung into the center of my head. My children, Gabby, then 7, and Sean, 5, often tiptoed into my bedroom, lay next to me, and spoke quietly about school and kid things. Shannon had just turned one. I read to them in a thin voice, wearing reading glasses for the first time: *The Giving Tree, The Missing Piece,* and *Thomas the Tank Engine* books—and during that time, I might have been the happiest person alive simply because I was alive.

One morning, I told Krista I wanted to watch a family movie later that night, which would be a milestone. It would mark the first time I walked down the stairs since my hospital release. Although each step would come like a Wisconsin logroller's unsteady attempts to stay upright, I knew Krista was strong, and I knew she had it in her to support me down the stairs.

A few memories remain from that night. As I sat in my favorite chair for the first time in a month, a sweet consolation overcame me; it was the first "normal evening" our family had experienced since I was rushed to the hospital. Owing to the walk downstairs, my head felt waterlogged for the duration of the movie. I remember my frustration at my inability to position my scarred head in a way that kept me from discombobulation. I don't recall the movie, but I remember wanting it to end shortly after it started. Despite the difficulties, I knew this was the first real day of my recovery. Soon, I would be walking Gabby and Shannon to the playground at the top of the street and throwing baseballs with Sean in the side yard.

I also remember Krista refilling her wine glass during the movie. I remember it well because of my strange reaction to the wine's odor, which revolted me. The wine carried the aroma of a household disinfectant. I knew my nerves were just beginning to knit back together and that my senses were in the process of resetting, so I didn't pay much mind to my revulsion. I did, however, remember Krista's consumption of wine, which was uncommon for her.

Despite the evening's aggravations, the night felt bathed in what seemed a Rockwellian warmth because my children—and Krista—knew I was on my way back.

Years later, I regard this night of resurrection as the evening when everything began to change in our home. It marked the night I first touched up against what seemed a looming shadow of an oppression in our home, one that became like a piece of furniture, an ironing board in the hallway closet, or the humming basement furnace.

Within a week, I was slowly walking down the stairs each morning to partake in a fine ritual. Since I had to relearn how to walk, my infant daughter unwittingly aided my therapy. Krista bundled Shannon up each winter morning and placed her in a stroller, where I then slowly pushed her through our neighborhood on sidewalks, which were often covered in snow. Passers-by smiled and waved. I never waved back, because I would have fallen to the ground; the counterbalance of the stroller was my crutch. My partially shaved head was hidden beneath my wool hat. I didn't know it then, but little Shannon would become a sacred anchor of consolation for me as life moved forward.

As I lay bedridden throughout most of that winter, I began to spend a great portion of my days in private thought, reflecting on my near-death experience and God's strange providence throughout my life. I recognized where He seemed often to allow pain and devastation into my life—infertility, adoption scams, my uncle's murder, an arthritic body, a failed right knee—to awaken me to His reality and love. I began to consider that perhaps the seeming tomahawk that thwacked into the back of my brain was actually another of God's attempts to activate a pause button on my life and bring me close to Him. Could God's love, perhaps even the best part of it, come with boxing gloves? Were my past pains His chiseling hands inside those fighting gloves? And was this violent form of love His best type of love and most powerful indication that He wanted me close to Him?

An abiding sense in me emerged that said, yes, God could—and often would—allow certain pains to bring me into greater conformity with His will. His love didn't seek consolation; it sought total intimacy. He wanted me to strive, hour-by-hour, minute-by-minute, to offer my life to Him, as a boy who strives to make his father proud. Near the end of my recovery, it began to become clear that God carried tender weapons to promote growth in virtue and total conversion. He would sparingly use them to draw whomever He could into His Kingdom. The confounding mystery of suffering, which has been atheists' blue-ribbon-prizewinning evidence for the absence of a benevolent God, seemed always to stoke renewal in me. It became clear in time: God's love *was*, in fact, violent—as violent as His longing to bring my soul into His Kingdom.

In the boredom of my recovery, while considering this mysterious way of His, I poured my thoughts into a book that later became *Burst: A Story of God's Grace When Life Falls Apart*. In the mini-memoir (I was too young and too immature to write a *real* memoir), I revealed brokenhearted tales of my flattenings and the manner in which God had masterfully remedied me.

By springtime, the elf in my head moved back to his dwelling place in Hell, and my headaches lessened. I could walk without Shannon's stroller. It was around then that I felt a deeper pull to God. When I finally was able to return to work, the world began to change for me. Old interests—DC politics, favorite television shows, and sports (except baseball)—began to lose some of their grip. I felt

myself becoming detached from myself and becoming sub-
sumed by His love.

Without verbalizing it, Krista told me much later that
she began to observe small changes in me. During those
moments when I began to share the horrors of the hospital, I noticed her subtle distance. I told her the manner
in which my sin and the overall state of my soul horrified
me as my body was laid in CT scanning tubes. I told
her of the demon-like characters that haunted me during
sleepless, hallucinatory nights on my neuro-ICU floor
and that I wanted to begin truly to center my life around
God's will.

Now and then, I posed questions that sounded lopsided
the moment they left my mouth: *What do you think holiness
looks like for us? . . . What do you think God wants our marriage
to resemble? . . . What sacrifices do we need to start making to help
get our kids into Heaven?* I am remembering now Krista's
reticence to engage; she often returned my thoughts with
sincere looks of puzzlement. Conversations related to God
and spiritual growth rarely gained traction—and because I
wanted this newness, and Krista didn't, an imperceptible
fissure in our marriage grew. Certainly, I realized my zeal
was raw and mostly still directionless, but her reluctance
even to engage was a mild disappointment to me. Eventually, when I noticed the air between us begin slowly to
decompress whenever I brought up matters of the soul, I
began to back off and keep my zeal private.

I also kept my confusion private. I had just managed
to make it through a medical event that many don't. I
was alive; which meant our marriage and family were as
well. In a sense, I was Lazarus lifted from the tomb. Killing
the fatted calf and a bit of merriment for what God had
done for us seemed appropriate to mark the time, but a
true spirit of jubilation never came.

At the time, I thought Krista was still in the despoliation of almost losing her husband. She had absorbed and seen horrific things at the hospital; watched doctors drill shunts into my head as skull dust floated in the air. She saw me hallucinate and continually sat by me as I lay in a comatose state. When I was lucid, she listened to me tell her of the demons that were swirling in the ceiling tiles. The hospital chaplain, Father Bill Spacek, told Krista he felt an oppression in my ICU room. She said she felt the same thing. Thereafter, the priest visited my room as many as three times a day to pray over me and scatter what he told Krista—and, much later, me—were small symphonies of demons encamped around my bedside. He held the Eucharist at the foot of my bed and commanded them to flee. Within the catacomb of my condition, I, too, found myself occasionally terrified by mysterious occurrences, demon-filled dreams, and frightening visions in my small hospital room that often seemed like a haunted house, where an unrestrained spirit had been set loose.

Throughout it all, Krista never left my bedside until she was asked to leave. At night, she slept on a small wooden chair in the lobby, where she often awoke in the lonely hours to look through the lobby door's glass panel to make sure my room was still dark. She had learned that a well-lit room during the late-night shift meant that surgeons were working wildly on a brain-affected patient. She watched the bodies of fully shrouded people be slowly pushed on gurneys out of the rooms on my floor. The seventh floor of neuro-ICU patients at the University of Maryland Medical Center is quieter than the moon.

Near the end of springtime, I was healthy enough to return to work. I was the vice president of our family's three-generation masonry contracting company that was loaded to capacity with projects. My first day back to work took me to my alma mater, DeMatha Catholic High School, where our company was performing the masonry work on a large new gymnasium.

Life quickly became a blur. Long workdays, kids' games, family time, and reuniting with friends had me where I was prior to the brain injury. Nothing really was the same anymore. My coordination and balance, and even the words coming out of my mouth, were minefields of struggle that needed to be navigated and patiently overcome. I intermittently slurred my words and, strangely, had trouble laughing. Bedtime came earlier. Each evening, weariness and fatigue overcame me at the winking of the first stars; I knew vessels in my head were reconnecting, and in time, a year or so, strength would begin to return. I had lost thirty pounds.

It was routine for me to leave for work before sunrise. One morning, I searched an odd cabinet in the kitchen where we stored a seldom-used coffee thermos. When I reached for it, I saw behind it an oversized jug of red wine, one of those fat wine carafes I remembered served as decoration on the top of hutches when I was a waiter at Little Italy in college. I remember being confused by the jug, but mentally categorized it as an old gift we had stowed away and forgotten about. I also remember that the jug was mostly empty. As I pulled my truck out of the driveway that morning, I didn't know the oversized carafe would mark the first of countless hidden bottles I'd find. In the summertime, bottles would be buried like empty caskets beneath the winter mittens and scarves. In the winter, wine bottles were stowed beneath beach towels, swimming goggles, and suntan lotions. They were tucked into high boots in the closet, rolled into seldom-worn flannel pajamas, hidden in backs of hutches, and placed like bottles of detergent in the shadowy, tight corner beside the washing machine.

Krista knew deep tides of pain from the onset of our marriage. We desired a large family, as many children as God would allow, but discovered quickly the fatal barrier of infertility would deny it. The awareness of our childlessness was a guillotine to our marriage. The gruesome stabbing murder of my uncle, Monsignor Thomas Wells, in his rectory one haunted night immediately followed. He was to be our benevolent guide throughout the agony of our infertility; he told us as much two nights prior to his murder, inside the same rectory where he was stabbed to death. He told Krista beneath the summer night's first stars, "I'll be here for you throughout it all." Adoption scams followed, including one in which the program director of our agency informed us, "Nothing I know of has ever happened on the scale of what happened to you. Not on *Dateline*, not on any news shows, not in my twenty years of doing this."

I was drawn deeply to Krista's gentle nature after meeting her in her Florida hometown. Unnaturally quiet, I quickly understood her soul was tethered to the small collection of horses she took care of in the small barn behind her home off a one-lane road in the flat Florida countryside. Krista had been a star hunter-jumper equestrian competitor on the Florida circuit. I remember seeing shoeboxes full of first-place ribbons and photographs of her soaring over four-foot-high jumps that she never mentioned to me.

One afternoon, I drove out to her house and saw her saddled on the back of Ariat, her favorite horse. When she saw me pull up in the distance, she steered Ariat through a gate in the meadow where dozens of cows grazed beneath canopies of live oak trees. She trotted beside me and strangely asked me to promise to stand still. Thereafter she lightly kicked her horse into a slow gallop where together they moved into a meadow more than a football field away.

When Krista finally turned back toward me, she was barely
a dot in the distance. Then, I heard a distant holler, and
within seconds, I marveled as Ariat and Krista became a
locomotive headed directly at me. I stood wonder-struck,
not knowing how to react to what seemed to be Secretariat
and his jockey bulleting down Belmont's stretch run—with
my body as the finish line. With the cadenced clomp of
Ariat at full gallop, headed directly at me, I remember my
only notion was to run. Then, about fifteen or so yards
from trampling over me, Krista subtly tugged the reins,
which her horse obeyed with a slight move to the side.
They whistled past me, missing me by no more than two
feet. It was horrifying. This was the day, the exact moment,
in fact, I fell in love with Krista.

I was fascinated by her work with horses. She used to
obtain Tampa Bay Downs' losing thoroughbred racehorses
and work to convert them into young children's future
hunter-jumpers. It was grueling work, which involved
breaking collections of nonwinning horses by teaching
them to quit doing all they had ever known: to break from
the gate and run. Krista knew the secret science of meek-
ing the speed still carved into their nature and instinct.
After taming and redirecting their spirits, she began to cre-
ate a new identity in the horses by teaching them to soar
over elegant arrangements of jumps. Many of the horses
were stubborn, but Krista was stubborn, too. She was born
naturally inclined toward gentleness and quietness, but she
became as mad as a bothered hornet when a horse bucked
her ways.

It was this stubborn streak that Satan identified as his
foothold—and in went his talons. In those early days, when
I began to speak to Krista about her drinking, her eyes
seemed to change form; the gentleness of her face seemed
to harden and become threatening. Her natural beauty and

gentleness of soul left her during those moments. In an instant, it was no longer my wife who stood in front of me; it seemed I was looking into the face of someone I no longer recognized.

When I summon memories of those early days, in the background remain the blurred images of my small children standing at the shoreline, looking to me to bring in their mom, a task of which I was incapable. Only God could rescue Krista from Satan.

Chapter 3

Darkness

With a clarity set in me like a lit candle left on a window ledge in the middle of the most frightening night of my life, I appraised where my soul stood before God. My flirtation with death brought a new call by God to come closer to Him.

Four days after an ambulance rushed me to the University of Maryland Medical Center, I was given my third CT scan. My medical team was failing in their attempts to embolize the blood trapped in my brain. On the occasion of this third scan, a contrasting agent was injected into one of my veins to enable doctors to get a better look into my fluid-crowded brain. At this seemingly loneliest point in my life, lying in the tube like a mannequin, I abruptly felt vomit rising in my throat. I had a bad reaction to the contrast. Because the brain injury took away my ability to speak or even move, I wasn't able to tell the medical team I was choking. It was then that my thoughts departed from my brain injury and turned to my other more urgent dilemma of choking to death. It was then, *right then*, that I considered God's imminent judgment of me and how things might unfortunately unfold.

I didn't love well enough.

God had given me the precious gift of Krista and our three God-delivered children, and it came to me at that haunting moment that I was somewhat lazy with my love. From the tube, which suddenly felt like a coffin, it seemed to me that my time in front of the throne of God would be, at best, indelicate. So I swallowed down my vomit—I wasn't eating, so it was mostly liquid—and, wide-eyed, I survived the event. When I was wheeled back into my room, I began to transition from thoughts of my damaged brain to thoughts of my eternal soul. When I saw Krista, I whispered in confused words for her and others to begin to pray for my soul. Shortly thereafter, a priest came in to hear my confession. The brain injury and cascading blood rendered my speech mostly incoherent. I found myself caught between the island of unconfessed sins and the graced countryside of absolution.

When, much later, I considered what actually unfolded that evening in the CT machine, it seemed to me that God had slipped me a secret invitation to encounter Him and His immensity. God had swung a lantern that shined too brightly into my soul that night, and I saw I wasn't the right material. The horror of my baggage, past sins, and laxity shamed me and clung to me like Hester Prynne's ineradicable letter. For the first time, a genuine fear of the Lord took hold. Hypertuned to my paper-thin mortality, I sensed God desired rapid advancement past my settled lifestyle. He had snatched me from myself that night and begun to rescue me from the clutches of the enemy swirling around my hospital room seeking to drag me to destruction.

When I left the hospital weeks later, I often found myself being involuntarily pulled into the furnace of His majesty. Due to that grace, I began to dedicate larger portions of my day strictly to God. As prayer and recollected inner silence became more consistent in my life, I felt myself journeying to untraveled places within me. Christ carried the torch, I followed along, and for the first time,

Jesus began to feel like a close friend. In time, I found myself wanting to annihilate all that was blocking the road to complete union with Him. His torchlight was leading me to *the pearl* of which He spoke. There is a price to be paid to be in an authentic relationship with Christ, and because I knew my post-surgery zeal would eventually fade, I understood conversion could only truly begin when I intentionally chose to die to myself and do my part to live only in Him. I needed to love well.

Certainly, this impulse to begin to pass through the purgative stage was a pure gift. He had planted the seed of this impulse just days before a surgeon opened the back of my skull. As I regained my health and began my return to normal life, a switchblade seemed to flick open in me, where a strange force within began to slice through and tear away the frontiers of distractions, vanity, lethargy, and sin to make more passable the narrow road to the pearl. An urgent desire compelled me to leave my commonplace life and to align it with the demanding will of God. I wanted to do things as He would have me do them—to begin to sacrifice joyfully for my family and pour my love into all others.

It was at this time that I began to enrich my relationship with Him with more frequent visits to my old parish for Eucharistic Adoration. As I traveled to construction sites throughout the day, I discovered the locations of nearby unlocked churches, where I would pull my truck over and open the door of an empty church that became a noiseless cell. As often as I was able, I'd kneel as close as I could to the Tabernacle, mostly to thank Him for sparing my life and to ask Him to help me become a worthy husband and dad.

Although I had always *known* God, attended Mass, received Him in the sacraments, and believed in His teachings, I had never fully permitted Him to engage my heart. For the first time, though, I began to regard the enormity of His majesty and paternal love. Noticeably, God began to make daily stops into my heart, like an old steam train that travels over high mountain ranges to deliver precious cargoes. I didn't know it then, but I was in the process of a transformation. I found His tenderness and mercies as bright Alleluias of hope, as emotion-charged as my first teenage doorstep kiss.

It was during this time that I became aware of an ancient prayer, the *Anima Christi*. I found myself praying it throughout the day, mouthing it in the Communion line, whispering it as I walked onto job sites, and praying it while I knelt before Mass. The single line that became an icon in me, the one that brought me to the rocks of Golgotha, was: *Within thy wounds, hide me. Suffer me not to be separated from thee.* The single line seemed to me the most charming, downhome, fireside manner to reach into the ferocious and sacred bosom of His heart.

I had no idea God had allowed me these strengthening graces to prepare me for what was to come.

In 2010, we lived in a corner brick house on a cul-de-sac in a pleasant neighborhood, where in the summertime our kids pedaled their bikes to the pool, ran through sprinklers, and explored the woods. They walked to the playground on top of the hill and sledded down larger hills in the winter. Most evenings after work, Sean and I played catch with the baseball in the side yard as neighbors taking evening strolls called out hellos. Gabby was often in the driveway making chalk drawings. Shannon was taking her wobbly first steps.

Krista would call us in for dinner, and every day felt full of life, as perfect as it could be after almost dying. We cheerfully engaged with the kids, and in those times, Krista shone with the quiet peace and settledness that once drew me to her. We loved and cared for one another as healthy married couples do; we freely exhibited small tokens of love. We'd often pray the Rosary after dinner and discuss the details of our days before Gabby and Sean headed upstairs for homework, baths, and bed. I'd hold Shannon and watch some of the Orioles' game.

Krista and I knelt each night to lead Gabby and Sean in bedtime prayers. Always at the end were my children's own intentions; the vulnerable words to God more tender than sunset at the sea. I'd close my eyes as they pulled their pure pleas to God from the kingdom of their imaginations. But as time moved on, I knew their voices marked for me what would usually become the night's final consolations, like the hooded abbot's final prayer for the transgressor whose head lay on the guillotine block. At the rise of the moon, a certain deadening would permeate our home. Krista would usually begin to watch a television show in which I had no interest, and I would begin to read.

Before heading to bed, I'd frequently ask Krista to join me upstairs. Although we spent the first ten years of our marriage routinely going to bed at the same time, now she rarely came upstairs with me. Often, she'd tell me she'd be up shortly. But I came to realize that after I left the family room and climbed the hardwood stairs, she wouldn't be sliding next to me until I was already deep into my dreams.

The brokenhearted routine took hold; a nighttime change in pattern that soon opened a howling loneliness that was like the slam of a heavy door closing on the night. As my eyelids drooped, Krista would be watching a reality television show and—as I would learn later—drinking red wine. I'd awaken before daybreak, usually around 5 A.M., and quietly walk from our bedroom to begin another day of being swallowed by the management of a dozen or so masonry jobs throughout the Washington, D.C., Beltway region and beyond.

Before I accepted my powerlessness within this new routine, I remember sitting with Krista at nightfall in the family room or on the back deck that looked out onto the small tree-enclosed English Garden. It was here where I often sat while recovering from brain surgery. On those nights, I mistakenly thought that sharing a glass of wine with Krista would show her the relaxed and proper manner of concluding a day. We would discuss the odds and ends of our days, chat about the kids, and plan out the next day. The surgery had done a number on my stamina and equilibrium, so fatigue would usually sweep over me by 9 P.M., and because my cerebellum had been sliced, my speech would slur, and a dull headache would often begin to set in. I wobbled when I walked. My surgeon told me that until blood vessels reconnected, I would be walking like "a drunken cowboy in a saloon" for a few years. Perhaps longer.

One day, when a third wine bottle turned up in an odd place, I placed it on our kitchen island. Krista wasn't home. When, later in the day, I saw the bottle no longer there, I told her we needed to talk. A stabbing memory remains of the "first discussion" about the hidden bottles. With the kids put safely off to sleep, I dipped my toe into a conversation in our family room.

"Krista, please tell me what is happening," I said.

"With what?"

With the bottle, the one I set on the island," I said cautiously. "I know you moved it."

She remained motionless, her eyes cast down. Neither of us spoke for several minutes. I remember thinking the silence was her pausing to piece together the right words to bare her soul. I recall hoping then that a wound would be exposed, that she would share a hidden shame causing her to drink in secret. I imagined, in the silence, soon holding Krista as she cried tears of secret pain trapped too long within her. I imagined looking at her through teary eyes and telling her we could overcome it together.

Finally, she spoke, "It's not a big deal. Why do you always make a big deal out of everything?"

I was caught flat-footed, my tongue completely tied. After failing to form a suitable response, I felt pulled into the vapor. "So a hidden wine bottle isn't a big deal?" I asked defensively.

"Don't attack me. Don't you dare attack me," she said in a tone I didn't recognize. She fell into a fixed squint. "It's like you're always searching for reasons to go after me."

Foolishly, I continued to think we were having an actual discussion and continued to engage (I didn't know the rules of the game yet, where Krista would masterfully and automatically flip a conversation about her drinking, isolation, and hidden bottles in the direction that put me in the wrong). "I'm not attacking you, Krista. I'm asking why the wine bottle was in the closet," I said, voice rising. "It's not the first bottle I've found hidden away."

"So, now you're spying on me," she said, seething. "Holy Kevin likes to spy on his wife. God must be really proud of you. Thanks for your concern. You really know how to show your love for me."

"I'm not spying on you," I said, already exasperated. "And I'm not on the hunt for bottles. The bottle was just there. Krista, what is going on?" Her response was confusing and hurtful, and I found myself caught like a boy lost in thick woods.

"All that's going on is you attacking me for putting a wine bottle where it shouldn't have gone," she defended. "I forgot I left it there. It won't happen again. Is that good enough for you?"

"Please, Krista, I don't care about the bottles. I only want to know if there's anything bothering you, anything you want to share with me?" I asked, softening. "Let's try our best to talk about it. We can work it out together."

"I'm not talking to you about anything," she fumed. Her eyes became slits. Time seemed to stop. After the pause in hostilities, she stood up and walked upstairs to our bedroom, where she locked the door. I slept on the couch. It was the first time in weeks she made it to our bedroom before me. I didn't make it at all.

I will never forget the fury of that first fight; when sheets of lightning seemed to rip open from the sky and wickedness filled the room. Our words struck me as spiritually cursed, as if a demon ventriloquist commandeered, tainted, and steered each one. I recall my own thoughts seeming impotent and incongruous, emerging from my mouth as if trying to pass through pea soup. Hers seemed animalistic and cut me to the core. Krista received my words as malicious personal rattlesnake strikes and immediately moved to delegitimize anything I said. I remember the *whoosh, whoosh, whoosh* of the ceiling fan seeming to pick up in intensity, its blades whirling just inches above me. As our voices rose, the walls seemed to sweat and push inward, and I wondered if Gabby and Sean had been awakened upstairs, cupping their ears to their bedroom doors.

The fight marked a sudden shift in chemistry between us. It was the night that reason and the loving language and matrimonial bond of a husband and wife began slowly to leak from our home. I witnessed a side of Krista I had never seen. She seemed guided by something that had removed her gentle nature, even taken hold of her being. With her now upstairs, I attempted to gather my wits and mentally take down the scaffold on what had unfolded. The fight seemed to act as a battering ram breaking past the doors of my brain that synthesized reason, order, and intellect. With that space suddenly vulnerable and unguarded, a stampeding, heart-pounding panic began to rush in. I felt concussed, as discordant emotions disgorged into me like unstoppable waterfalls. I couldn't get a hold of any logical or even plausible explanation for how quickly the fight spiraled. I lay on the couch, wide-eyed. As my mind began to settle, I began to pray to God that He would resolve what happened by the next day, but I knew that something had been torn away that evening. I sensed even then it would never come back.

That was the evening when everything changed in our marriage and home.

That fight became the template for each that followed when another hidden bottle turned up, or when I shared how her habits were splitting us apart. I didn't know the Olympian magnitude of Krista's deep well of shame or that emancipation from her wounds was not only secret drinking—but me. Wine was the shame-killing elixir; *I* was the release—the catch-all reservoir for the fallout of the following day's humiliation and disgust with herself. The dynamic never occurred to me back then: Krista hated what she was doing to herself, did it anyway, and purged herself of the ignominy as quickly as she could— directly upon me—the following day. Looking back on those early days and at the haze of my feeble attempts to pull her from the sarcophagus of her drinking, I see a clear image of myself as a small boy turned around and lost, walking deeper into the wrong direction of a forest.

I was not fully aware at the time—or, at least in the depths of me, I refused to acknowledge it—that she was drinking most nights. I do remember this thought, and I imagine it is common for others in my situation. I attributed the dark period to a bad phase that would eventually repair itself through introspection and self-awareness. One day, it would become piercingly clear to her, I innocently and hopefully thought back then, that she was failing as a wife and mother. It would be on that day that she would begin to break through the hard frost of her habits and fully return to the family that loved her.

My gravest and most grievous mistake was failing to understand, or even appreciate, the weight of Krista's shame. She carried enormous wounds from her childhood, indelible icons of feeling unloved and rejected. Satan knew it, and he would press harder and harder into her shame as she grew older.

In my naïveté and with no roadmap or definitive plan to help her through the disquieting obstacles of her shame and woundedness—I remember daily giving Krista wholly over to God, forcing myself to trust that He would tend to her in due time. But time was moving on, and the pattern of dysfunction was hardening.

Her late-night drinking marked our boundaries. If I let it go, things were fine in our home, at least as it was seen from the outside. I knew enabling the dark habits created a weak man who had opened the door to disorder. So with the layers of her woundedness always in mind, I persisted in conversationally wading into the dark pools of her binge drinking, where Krista consistently shifted into an amalgam of incongruous justifications. When I resisted her illogical logic, blitzkriegs rained down, and the piecemeal disintegration of our marriage continued its course. After some time, I felt the part of the blood-stained boxer in the late rounds who rises from his corner stool and stumbles punch-drunk into another storm of violent combinations. I would eventually head up for bed, where I would often later awaken with Krista next to me, knowing she had slipped beside me while I slept, more in love with television and wine than me. I remember a rippling of runaway adolescent-like brokenheartedness churning in me, where

I felt like a jilted teenage boy whose first high-school crush had dumped him.

The peculiar zig-zagging pattern in our marriage calcified. Daytime hours were mostly normal in our home; but the sinking of the sun spawned an otherworldly atmospheric mood change. A quiet darkness seemed to pass through each room, like black mold that expands on the unseen side of basement walls. The rise of the moon became a magnet for tension and more awkward and inelegant conversations.

As Krista began to grow distant in the evenings, I found myself sitting close to her holding a magazine or book, or watching a baseball game, internally asking myself the typical questions of a troubled marriage: Had I done something to cause her to fall out of love? Was I spending too much time at work? Was loneliness causing her to drink? Depression? Why did she hold such simmering anger for me? Was she exhausted with me and what maybe she regarded as weakhearted attempts to bring us closer? Was she no longer attracted to me—bored with me? Was I failing to love her well as a husband, failing at being the man she deserved? *Was I the reason she was drinking?*

When I did speak, I told her I deeply missed her, that I needed her. "If there's anything I need to know, anywhere at all where I'm letting you down," I said, internally pleading for there to be something for me to do to make this go away, "... let me know what it is. I'll fix it." Her clipped responses usually contained a deadened detachment, like I was speaking a different language from a land far across the ocean. After some time, she just seemed to find me bothersome. Her eyes registered nothing. So I'd get up from the chair in the family room and unceremoniously head up to bed.

A new routine began for me. After climbing the stairs for sleep, I'd carefully open my sleeping children's bedroom doors, walk to their bedsides, where they became like candlelight that burned away the psalms of lamentations wringing my heart. The gentle in-and-out rhythm of their breath spoke in my soul like the whispery AM static of the transistor radio that lulled me to sleep as a child. As moonlight shone through their windows, I mouthed pleading words to God to protect them from the harm of a troubled marriage and the addiction that had invaded our home. With tears often welling, I begged Him to bring them peace and their mom back to the quietude and settledness of her former days. *Take pity on her, Lord; she is ill. These children need their mom. Things are collapsing. Turn your eyes to Krista and end this. Listen to me, God. Heal her. Bring her back.* The nighttime custom then became the abiding rhythm of my life and offered me then what became an unbreakable grip on hope.

Saint Paul's ancient reminder to the newly betrothed about love's demands played like an old-time radio show on those perturbed nights: "Love bears all things, believes all things, hopes all things, endures all things" (1 Cor 13:7). The words were a toehold, a sacred map, and a compass. As time stretched on, it was Paul's final word on *endurance* that I clung to, as a drowning man strains for a passing shipwreck. As Paul began to make do with his intractable thorns, I felt that I, too, needed to prepare for a long trial just in bloom. The wounds and strange patterns were expanding, like rare and grotesque-smelling flowers. To endure these movements, I had to adjust my thinking and put on the big-boy trousers of a Depression-era longshoreman gathering crates with a mangled hand—who mouths winced prayers to God to get him to dusk and back to his tenement to feed his family. I had no idea then of how little I knew and of the measures required of me.

As I knelt by my children, I looked at the lids of their dreaming eyes and saw them as small lambs, vulnerable and left exposed to the fallout of marriage in travail. Everything was unhidden now; they were just too young to understand. But in that silence, I did viscerally feel Christ's presence, almost as if He had knelt beside me to enter into my Gethsemane, where He served in a twofold fashion: for me, He sweated the Garden blood of His submissive will. For my children, He breathed into their sleeping souls His protecting Spirit, one that I imagined traveled to the hollows of the unprotected places in them—the places where a strange new awareness of something being wrong was building.

As I sought to accept my chalice in Gethsemane, I began lavishly to offer fasts from food on hand-picked days and committed to a number of self-denials. I began small mortifications, like refraining from reaching for the cell phone at stoplights. I often drove from job to job with the radio turned off, rejected sweets and cream and sugar in my coffee, and suffered through occasional lukewarm and cold showers. I strove to practice patience and manifest joy with recalcitrant site superintendents and employees who showed up late for work. My Rosaries and supplications intensified. At the same time, I foolishly imagined that increasing my tenderness for Krista—putting on a cheerful face and offering unseen acts of love—might coax from her a return to settled peace. I still thought her healing depended on me.

My memory flashes to a night when I told Krista I thought she had built her entire life around drinking alone at night. When she remained stone-faced, I deepened my resolve to unburden all that was in my mind and stepped farther in. I told her that her nighttime drinking was taking over her life and that she should seek help or stop altogether. I offered to unite myself fully with her and vowed to join her in abstaining from alcohol. I told her I would attend every AA meeting with her. It was at this suggestion that I came to understand the pitiless and untamed grip wine had. She transformed, it seemed to me, into what seemed a desert dust devil, swirling into a sustained attack, claiming that all I did was cast judgment on her. From the beginning of our marriage until now, she said I had searched for ways to criticize her. "How dare you judge me and what I do when you go to bed," she screamed. Her vitriol was a mushroom cloud. "Poor little Saint Kevin. The saint who never does anything wrong. The little saint who goes to bed by himself," she mocked while pantomiming bows with hands clasped in prayer. "Get away from me—and stay away from me. And I will never go to a meeting, because I don't need one!"

Magnificent despair covered me then. Her mockery, denials, and dark-heartedness revealed a mind and a soul at war. But reader—do not let yourself be hoodwinked by the poor husband who holds the pen of this narrative. Let it be unambiguously clear that my execution and tone often fell far short of the standard of a husband wanting to help free his wife from her interior pain. My words, too, cut deep, and I'm certain on some nights Krista saw me as her greatest enemy, for which I can't blame her.

Within the crackling heat of some of our arguments, I remember becoming aware of something unfolding: As our tempers flared, I palpably felt Satan's power broadening. Each word seemed to open up more ground to burrow deeper into our marriage. Although I could not hear it, I could *feel* the croak of his amusement. It was an inaudible throbbing that poured into our family room, that bounced off the walls like an echo of his riotous crowing in Gethsemane.

Month followed month, during which I stayed true to my offerings and prayer. I was uncomprehending, though, of the oceanic depth of her vice. The time-tested Catholic

remedies began to feel hollowed out, deprived of all spiritual power against the toxic weight of her secret shame
and wounds. At the time, habitual nights with red wine
seemed to me even more powerful than God. My prayers,
fasts, and mortifications seemed to act as accelerants to the
disorder. I can look back now—and likely did then—and
see that I repeatedly served as my own enemy. Although
in prayer I stretched myself repeatedly to surrender Krista
to God, admitting my helplessness, there were times when
my vigilance weakened and occasionally collapsed in the
face of another "bad night." I too easily allowed discouragement to diminish my faith in God. *My* hangover from
a "bad night" filtered like nitroglycerin into my bloodstream as a murderer of hope.

As the pattern firmed, I began to make plans to arrange
for an intervention and finally to share the pain with my
siblings. But at the last minute, I canceled, deciding to
bottle everything up and continue to face the grief alone.
In my heart—but not my mind—I remained resolute that
Krista would heal through God and find her way back
over the far mountains with a shepherd holding her hand.
While I clung to God more fiercely than ever, He seemed
as far away as Krista.

I began to read books on alcoholism. I met with two
counselors to gain insight into what I might be able to do.
The responses kept coming back the same: it is up to your
spouse alone to stop. Loving consideration and patience
with Krista are understandable, but your intent will always
be overwhelmed by her pull to binge drink at night. For
the first time in my life, I confessed despair in the confessional. When the priest probed, I told him my wife had
taken up the habit of secretly drinking, which was beginning to impact our family. He echoed the counselors, but
was more frank. He said that until my wife sought help,

the clutch of our family would fragment and begin a free-fall. I left the confessional with my head on fire and my soul in a seeming casket.

One morning, while managing a large masonry project for our company, I saw that there was a Catholic counseling service across the street. I met with the counselor and explained my situation. I told her I tossed and turned each night worrying about Krista and that I was consumed with worry that her drinking was beginning to spread like an infection into my family. She offered some professional advice on how to help persuade Krista to join me to meet with her. She warned: *Do not speak of alcohol; speak only of wanting to help your marriage.*

A week later, Krista surprisingly agreed to meet with her. The counselor focused solely on our marriage the first two meetings, and Krista seemed moved by her wisdom and the suggestions she gave navigating the issues of a troubled, but still Christ-centered, marriage. Midway into our third meeting, the counselor turned her chair to Krista and calmly asked, "Krista, do you find that alcohol presents a stumbling block to loving Kevin well as his wife?" The question dropped into the room like a pheasant shot mid-flight from the sky.

Krista stared for a moment into the unblinking, grave eyes of the counselor, who had just trespassed on the sacrosanct, then dropped her head and stared into the beige carpet. After some time, Krista raised her eyes, blurry with tears, and turned to me. From her underground rivers of pain burst forth just two words, *I'm sorry*. Then she wept. I pulled my chair close and held her, as tears began to well in my eyes. Memory doesn't permit, but I imagine something like Barber's *Adagio for Strings* began to resound in me. The counselor brought over a box of tissues. For several minutes, the only sound in the room was Krista's weeping. When she regained her composure and straightened herself, she smiled and looked at the counselor. "Yes," she said in a thin voice. "Drinking wine at night was a problem."

The counselor looked at Krista with the warmth of the Blessed Mother and said, "Thank you, Krista, for being vulnerable." She reached into her purse and turned to me with a $10 bill. "We're going to stop early today," she said to me. "When we meet next, we'll go over what's just come up. For right now, though, it's more important for the two of you to walk across the street to the coffee shop and talk about what Krista just shared. So get out of my office and enjoy the coffee—my treat."

Holding hands, we crossed a busy downtown Bethesda street and sat down at a small table, where Krista quietly shed more tears. For the first time, she apologized for her drinking and for not loving me well. She said she would get a hold of her late-night habits and begin to work hard to love me and our family. We discussed the future and shared our hopes. She shared that she wanted to live up to her full potential and flourish as a wife and mother. Her eyes shone with a tender contradiction of enormous shame and a willingness to overcome herself and work to love me.

Krista shared some about the wounds of her past, then asked me to help her get through them. She told me that she loved and missed me. She kissed me, a kiss of Heaven, looked me in the eyes, and said nothing else.

It was at that corner table that I felt like a small boy again, the wide-eyed, innocent version of me—the boy who flung off his jacket at the first hint of springtime as the old mysterious bond of sacramental matrimonial grace covered me whole.

After a week of settled peace and a return to her former joyful ways, Krista stayed downstairs one night. We were scheduled to return to the counselor the following day.

The counselor never saw us together again.

I pleaded with Krista about returning—reminding her about her vow to meet her full potential—but I was met with dark silence and intransigence. Drinking had become an immutable part of her soul, as greed ruled in Judas Iscariot.

I went back to the counselor alone, explaining what had happened. She looked at me with the shattering tenderness of my pitying mom. Behind her eyes, I saw a Dostoevsky-like novel portending what she perceived as coming marital devastation. I'll never forget the death knell look reflected in her eyes, nor will I forget her wordlessness.

Within a few weeks, Krista and I had become like slow-moving tectonic plates moving past one another. It was around that time that on that same construction project, I overlooked a detail on the structural section of the blue-prints that cost our company a few thousand dollars. As a remediation company came in with ear-splitting jackhammers, huge drills, and large masonry saws to cut through our recently laid cinder block, I wept in an unfinished corner of the building like a boy who'd lost his parents at a fair.

In the meantime, until the masonry on that large condominium project was completed, I drove past the corner table in the coffee shop and thought of Krista, who had stepped into a distant countryside where her footsteps couldn't be tracked. She was in a land I couldn't enter.

Chapter 4

Moving Nowhere

We moved from our corner house into a rancher five miles away with a large open field and a narrow stream in the backyard; where fox and deer seemed to gather each night. Krista picked the house because of its semi-country seclusion and the opportunity to stall a horse in the field. She looked at me earnestly and said she would work to get healthier here, and a sliver of optimism in me grew. The pastoral setting, I hoped, would remind Krista of the tender wholesomeness of her teenage years so often spent riding a horse on wide-open Florida scrubland. I hung a thick-roped swing on the strongest branch of the enormous American elm tree in our new front yard. As I played with my children in that yard, I began to push them as high as I could, imagining a new season, like the promise that floats in the breezes above Florida baseball diamonds in the early days of March.

A few days after the moving truck unloaded, I carefully hand-selected and laid one hundred or so large gray, silver, slate, and gold-colored field stones into the bed of my pick-up. At home, I wheelbarrowed the stone out to the middle of a garden in our backyard, where a Marian grotto would soon be built. I sketched out a design and handed it to a stone mason who smiled and quietly told me he had a devotion to Mary. I requested he angle the grotto, so it appeared that the blue-robed visage of Our Lady of Lourdes was craning her body from the niche to look into the back of our home with affection and maternal care. I dug up dirt and planted small rose bushes around the stone and imagined our family soon praying Rosaries there. I found a small light that bathed Mary in soft light throughout the night. I didn't know then how her gaze from the illuminated grotto would serve me in the same fashion as my old childhood nightlight that scattered the darkness.

Our parish, Our Lady of the Fields, was close to our home, so close in fact that we could walk through our back field, pass a few houses, bear to the right, and step through the church's front doors in the time it took to pray three decades of the Rosary. Perhaps because of the church's proximity, I volunteered to become more active at the parish and helped to start a men's group. I joined a prison ministry and facilitated some Scripture studies, all of which Krista wholeheartedly encouraged; I didn't know then of the dark new dynamic that was taking shape. Upon my return home from time spent at the parish, Krista would often be asleep. As I lay down for bed, a thin odor of wine often passed over me.

As the pattern of the sharp hot-Windex odor of wine took hold, I told Krista I no longer had a desire to spend time at the men's group. When she balked, complaining that I didn't spend enough time with friends, I told her that I knew she was drinking when I was away. She told me to "stop trying to control her"—the latest of the hydra-headed slogans to eliminate an attempt to bring things back to order. If I managed to cut off the head of one "slogan" by helping her to see its fiction—and how her isolation and secret consumption of wine was hurting us—another head of a seeming wild boar or serpent would pop up in its place.

Most evenings, though, I was home with Krista and the kids, where the pattern established in the old house stayed true. After the kids headed off to bed, an uneasy silence began to stretch between us as Krista began her slide back into the chill of her nighttime cloister. She wouldn't come to bed until late, when I was already asleep. If I awakened, I too often smelled the wine.

On many of those nights, when I didn't feel even a particle of hope, I reached into the drawer of my bedside table for a bottle of holy water and began to anoint and pray over Krista's sleeping body. But even as I unscrewed the cap and quietly walked into the darkness by her side of the bed, I mostly felt a crumbling hopelessness. On some nights, I found myself dismissing both the gesture and the efficacy of the anointing, regarding it as a hocus-pocus Catholic flinging of tap water.

There were two nights, though, that changed my thinking. On those occasions, as I sprinkled the blessed water onto Krista and asked God to mix in His saving blood, a sudden chill enveloped me, like a miner stepping into a sudden pocket of cold air. It seemed I had stepped past the thin borderland of an in-between place, where a door had been opened to a sensation of malevolence. Perhaps it was my tiredness, but an unearthly presence seemed to graze close beside me. Our bedroom was perfectly still when Krista's soft breath became what sounded like soft and imperceptible wheezings and otherworldly murmur-ings. My breath left me then, and the hair follicles on my forearms stood on end. The darkness of Krista's isolation had magnetically drawn in evil. I imagined in those ghastly moments then that if someone had flicked on the light, I would have glimpsed the scattering of black flapping wings. It became clear to me that the anointing of my poor Krista on those spine-tingling nights was perhaps the most powerful thing I could do. But really, outside of prayer, it was also all I actually knew to do.

On other nights when Krista still hadn't come to bed, I'd awaken from fitful sleep and look through the rear door of our bedroom where I would see Krista watching television and drinking wine. The previous owner designed the rear of our rancher with large ceiling-to-floor windows to capture sunlight. Because our master bedroom extended out from the rest of the house, I could lift a few blinds and look directly into the family room. Although the image wearied me, I didn't divert my gaze. *Seeing it*, I thought then, would act as a catalyst for me to fight harder for her and be more imaginative in creating ways to bring her to an awareness of the harm of her drinking. Standing like a voyeur in the dark, I debated whether or not to attempt dialoguing with Krista in those moments. I often knelt on the hardwood and told God what was in my head and asked that He reorder my thoughts so they would cohere and blaze light into Krista's conscience when I left the room to speak with her. In that place of dim hope—God's words never came. Filled with the inner tension of the fecklessness of former approaches she always viewed as sabotage, I slid back into bed and asked God to pass His words of love and order into her.

Newly hatched stratagems for dialogue and persuasive arguments to address the drinking began always to feel prematurely doomed. Whenever I spoke to her about the wine and her solitude, I felt like I dropped onto a black-diamond slope of sheer ice with bunny-slope ability. Her responses, no matter how carefully I planned or mentally went over them beforehand, came back clipped and angry and cast me in the part of the choleric southern prohibitionist preacher, whose bombast from the high pulpit moves congregants to want to tilt the bottle all the more.

It had arrived at the point where my words were always resisted and turned back on me. Any conversation that involved her drinking spiraled into the devil's plaything.

Wearied and finding sleep difficult, a consoling routine began. As the sheet music of bachelor crickets and courting bullfrogs poured through the screen window into a bedroom that began to feel like the plains of Nineveh, I'd prop myself up on pillows and bedstand and gaze out at the illuminated statue of Mary. It served as a nightlight then, like the flickering light of an old oil rig that warms the imagination of a boy growing up in a gulf town.

Mary's hands extended past the folds of her blue robe, and I always imagined them extending out to me, as a mother reaches for her wounded child. The image of her solitary presence in the darkness of the night was medicine poured into me. She, too, suffered agony; far more than I. I prayed the Sorrowful Mysteries then, where in my Irish imagination I allowed Mary to take my hand and lead me, decade by decade, into blood-stained landscapes. From Gethsemane to her Son's nailing and death, she was casting floodlights into my soul, reminding me of the manner in which I must commit in order to conquer disorder and darkness. As Our Lady clung to God in embracing the strange plan for the salvation of mankind, I, too, was being asked to shoulder a hated and despised cross and continue to trust in God's love and the hope for Krista's healing.

With my head turned to the left toward the grotto, I imagined Mary's eyes riveted to the mayhem heaped upon her Son. Although she witnessed evil, she never took her eyes from it. Even though she periodically fell onto her knees, she knelt in the mud as a genuflection to the mystery of the Cross. She was carving into me an icon of what surrender to the God of a broken heart resembles. She was trying to pass on to me the sacred blueprint of the thousands of suffering saints down the years, who took on crucified lives in abandoning themselves to His care. Unlike the Mother of God, though, none of the saints actually knelt at the literal heart of the mystery of the Cross. As she held my hand, in her humble way, she was showing me that she went through Hell, survived, and later opened her door to see her Son standing there. "Kevin, Krista will come back in the same way," Our Lady seemed to be telling me, "if you live out your cross and surrender everything to my Son."

As thoughts of Our Lady of Lourdes' visage melted into me on those nights, I asked her to repair the injury in my soul and build in me a hope that I knew I lacked. In the moments before sleep, I did what I had learned to do as a child and gave my Rosary to my angel. *Go to God as a beggar* was my last plea of the night.

Most mornings, I knelt in darkness at my bedside and looked at Krista asleep beneath thick covers. Sleep usually managed to replenish the empty wells of the prior night. Propelled by my deep love for her and desire to protect her, I quietly renounced the demons of wine and shame and then asked God to reveal His will within the despoliation of my marriage. I begged for the wisdom of understanding the true path that would finally free her. Before getting ready to leave for work, a handful of existential questions emerged in the dark wood of my mind: *How do I help/love/serve my wife in her enslavement? What is my duty and God's will as her husband? How do I die for her to help promote healing when she has repeatedly rejected it?*

Answers never came; in fact, all that ever really came was the thought to continue practicing the customary Catholic heirlooms of prayer, fasting, and the practice of charity in the home. Other than that, it became evident that I had no idea what God's plan was for me. A heavy tarpaulin, it seemed to me, was beginning to separate me from the world.

Because a few months earlier I had held out a measure of hope for what Krista promised about a new start, those early days in our new home felt like the beginning of a long penance. I began to see the wine as a savage *destroyer* of both Krista and me; a poisonous and fast-moving cloud burning out the lungs of our souls. I found myself becoming mortally afraid then, because I didn't know how to stop it or stop her from buying or drinking it. She had hopscotched around, moving from liquor store to liquor store, to disguise her addiction. Besides prayers and dependence on God, I didn't know how to fight Satan for my wife. I remember praying with greater urgency then, but as the old pattern once more solidified in our new home, my pleas began to feel despairing and disorderly, like a seaman who fires a flare that zigzags chaotically into the sea; a brief blaze of light that no one sees.

It was always in the air, the wine, the weight of my powerlessness, Krista's ringed eyes, the growing chasm between us, the silence, and the flickering out of the easy joy and laughter from earlier days. The pain of my arthritic knees became ratcheted up, and the shine of my eyes dulled. I had even begun to take on Krista's same characteristics and patterns. Restless sleep came in snatches for both of us. Our bones ached in the morning, and we both carried slight dark circles beneath our eyes. Brain fog slowed our thoughts, lifting periodically throughout the day. She stayed quieter; I did, too. Even when we were alone, we felt overcrowded. A *pressing-down* sensation trailed me, and I imagine it did for Krista, too, from room to room. I didn't feel at ease anywhere—at work, among friends, at Mass and prayer, or even among my children. I imagine we shared equally in the sensation of having entered a swallowing solitude that was hollowing us out. In differing ways, the feeling of desolation had become imperialistic for us both. Simply, we had become exhausted.

As time stretched on, we seemed to pass by one another underwater. I remember always getting into my truck before dawn, pulling out of the driveway, and pounding the steering wheel. As I made my way through the starlit-covered neighborhood and onto Route 50 toward downtown Washington to begin another work day, I prayed the Rosary and pleaded with Mary to mother Krista back to health. I *knew* Christ could heal Krista, and I held on fiercely to what Beloved John wrote: "And this is the confidence which we have in him, that if we ask anything according to his will he hears us. And if we know that he hears us in whatever we ask, we know that we have obtained the requests made of him" (1 Jn 5:14–15). John's reminding words were an emollient to my soul, but it was the loneliest psalm that always played loudest in me: "Incline your ear to my cry! For my soul is full of troubles, and my life draws near to Sheol. I am reckoned among those who go down to the Pit; I am a man who has no strength, like one forsaken among the dead, like the slain that lie in the grave, like those whom you remember no more, for they are cut off from your hand. You have put me in the depths of the Pit, in the regions dark and deep. Your wrath lies heavy upon me, and you overwhelm me with all your waves" (Ps 88:2–7).

It had come to this: encouraging Krista to a healthier manner of living had grown stale for both of us. It had devolved into a chump chase. She had been given the faculty of free will, and as the scabs of her woundedness thickened, I knew scars of cynicism and anger were becoming indelible in me. My prayers then always seemed immediately dumped into a boneyard of dead and ignored

petitions. Bereft of any recourse, I told Krista one night
that I would be abstaining from all alcohol. A darkness
passed over her eyes. After pausing, she said with derision.
"The holy one strikes again," she said. "Too good for a
beer now. Do whatever you want."

After a period of silence, the old fight came back, like
a familiar prepackaged fever dream. The velocity of the
back and forth came on like a cyclone, and I knew we
were back on the familiar carnival ride. Her glacial squint
returned, the floors dropped, and my stomach tightened.

Month followed month, and I began to consider my life
differently. It was the first time in my life when I felt little
more than my brokenness. I felt myself becoming more
solemn at work and around friends and stopped believing
in joy in the method I had always known. The pleasure
of watching Gabby's high steps at Irish dance, the swing
of Sean's aluminum bat, or a walk into the woods with
Shannon would in all likelihood be abrogated by a rupture
later that evening. Interior *why-me, why-Krista* questions
no longer meant anything to me. When I did speak to
God, it was mostly just to ask how to sustain some measure
of hope within what seemed to have become a marital
crucifixion. But He never told me. So, in that silence, I
kept a close eye on the kids and worked to keep them as
closely tethered as I could to their ancestral right to won-
der, innocence, and order.

At night, I no longer bunched my pillows to look for
Mary.

Our marriage grew quieter. I wouldn't ask Krista to
leave the home, and she knew I would never leave. As
the days stretched on, Krista's isolation and binge drinking had taken on a permanence. Within the piteous time,
red tides of taunts became shrill in my mind: *You're stuck
with her. It's killing your family. Krista can't stand you. God
is dead in this, and she will drink tonight.* As Satan mocked

polyphonically, God, it seemed, didn't even whisper. I felt the power of evil strengthening in my home.

I often took back roads on drives home from work, where I would climb the winding road that took me to the old hilltop graveyard at Sacred Heart, one of America's oldest chapels. I'd get out of my truck and sit beneath the longest branch of a mammoth oak tree that seemed to point in the direction of my uncle Monsignor Tom Wells' gravestone fifteen feet away. Time seemed to collapse there as memories of him cheered me. Since pedaling my little green bike to his rectory in Bowie, Maryland, as a seven-year-old, I had grown up in his shadow and traveled the world with him. There was very little he didn't know about me, and I knew a lot about him.

I recall autumn evenings when the sun slipped beneath the tall golden- and red-leafed trees that seemed to wrap as protective mother bears around hundreds of tombs. I took my normal spot on the ground in front of his grave and bared my soul, which felt as ground to dust as the disintegrated bodies all around me. I spoke aloud to him like a lost child, posing questions in the open as if he were alive, his legs leisurely kicked out and head and back inclined against the cold stone of his own grave marker. *Man, Tommy, what do I do with this? What does God want? Where do I even start to get this right? Tommy, do I just step away?* I tried to summon the wisdom he'd imparted to me so many times down the years, piecing together fragments of old conversations that had dimmed over time. Mostly, the only words that came were: *Keggy, this is the cross. One day Jesus will take it away, just not now. Nail yourself to this cross. Peace will come to Krista and you—and the demons will die— when you live on the cross and patiently trust God.*

As became customary, I asked that he help bear the weight of what felt like a steady collapse of my marriage,

nature, and peace of soul. I spoke frightening things to
him, words he had never heard from me while he was
alive. I told him I was losing trust in God, which I knew
he would have regarded as a dooming third-rail admission. If he could have reached his arms from the grave to
my disconsolate body, I imagine he would have grabbed
me by the collar with one hand and slapped me with the
other, attempting to startle me back to reason and faith.
He built the entire foundation of his priesthood on total
dependence on God. I pleaded that he ask God to stir up
resilience in me. On some nights, as I drove from the cemetery to head the rest of the way home, I wept because I
had no map out of the pain.

As the pattern became stubbornly predictable, worms
of guilt and recrimination began to tunnel into me. I felt
I was doing nothing to help Krista become well. In time,
it became clear to me that I had played a part in Krista's
pain—and I would have to render an account to God. She
had hardened, but so had I.

Following "bad nights," I often arrived home from
work carrying an Arctic silence, even though I knew Krista
subconsciously screamed for me to walk through the door
as a merciful and understanding man. Although I prayed
at various parts of the day for wisdom and forbearance, I
sometimes behaved at home as seemingly having prayed
for the opposite. I was living out the insidiousness of Paul's
admission to the Romans in real time: "So then it is no
longer I that do it, but sin which dwells within me. . . . I can
will what is right, but I cannot do it. For I do not do the
good I want, but the evil I do not want" (Rom 7:17–19).

There were promising stretches when Krista emerged
like Lazarus bright-eyed from the tomb, but instead of lav-
ishing her with affirmation and the hope that burned in
me, I often tacked toward reservedness. Even as Krista's

eyes shone with a glint of promise, mine, I imagine, looked guarded. There were days when she looked into my eyes for a safe port and didn't find one. Looking back, I see that I wasn't Thomas, who doubted; I was Judas, who betrayed. My tiredness with the patterns and detachment had made me an unwitting collaborationist in festering the pus in her wounds. Even though I knew it was up to Krista to quit her habits, I began to see how I was contributing to keeping the rock at the entrance of her tomb.

I began to explore the dark corners in me that perhaps I had conveniently neglected when Krista began to drink secretly. I began to contemplate my soul before God, where awareness and humiliation covered me like an acid bath. He became alarmingly alive, and suddenly—before the furnace of His gaze—there were no barriers or hiding places. I became aware of clusters of graceless gestures, lazy omissions, and resentments, but the garment really began to tear and come apart when I pulled the strings of fidelity and sacrificial love. I knew Krista would never fully heal until I *chose* to love her without cost.

Colorfast images of my marital failures darted into my mind like great white sharks that bump the under-side of rafts. As my shame grew, I tried to deconstruct the many false narratives, tactical errors, and flawed edifices of thought in which I had bracketed myself from Krista's wounds. As a former journalist trained to investigate, I cautiously stepped into the unvisited places in me, and began to force myself to lift and look beneath untouched rocks. Thereafter, in those places, I opened up inquisitional deluges, hoping that probing questions would clear pathways to loving my suffering wife as God willed.

Was I loving Krista poorly? Within the never-ending Passion play of our nightly isolation, had I selfishly allowed my aggravation to sever our matrimonial vows? Was I telling myself comforting lies about the manner in which my prayers and sacrifices were more efficacious than tender looks, loving touches, or instantaneous embraces by the kitchen island? Had I lazily given up trying to reach the untouchable and mysterious places in her?

Was I more consumed with Krista's wounds than with the sunny memories from our past? Had I allowed amnesia to blanket my hope, where I no longer recalled Krista's quiet nature and gentleness that once pulled me to her like a magnet?

What were my underlying motives for keeping the binge drinking a secret? Was it actually a sickness *inside of me—my* own shame that I had chosen to bury from public view? When I left for work each morning, why did I behave as if all was well? Was it a coping mechanism or a vein of pride? Why did I fight against becoming vulnerable and sharing my pain with a small group of close friends and siblings? Was my silence a noble act to keep from adding to Krista's shame—or did I keep everything hidden to prevent my family from being stigmatized? Was I just postponing an inevitable collapse to maintain order in my family?

Did the witness of my own drinking initiate her destructive habits? Why was I still drinking the occasional beer or having a glass of wine? Did I set the table for her binge drinking when I drank my pints when we dated?

Was I betraying my marital vow to demand her admittance into a rehabilitation clinic? Was it an effeminate strain in me that kept me from drawing definitive lines? Why was I awakening each day juggling balls of situational ethics rather than drawing the blood a man must in making firm decisions? Had I become the cowardly soldier who, instead of running toward the chaos, runs for the hills at the first rifle shot?

Was it a demonstration of hope or insanity to hand Krista fully over to God, even at a point where my two eldest children might recognize the patterns behind Mom's woundedness? With no guideposts, professional help, or an elaborate plan to help, I surrendered to the saving love and mercy of God. Within a wilderness of years of seemingly dead-letter prayers, though, the act of surrender was beginning to seem senseless.

Early each morning, I took the kaleidoscope of untidy images and interrogations to pre-dawn prayer and began an Ignatian Examen seemingly birthed and guided by a demon. I always lit a candle and placed it on the window ledge across from me to soothe me. But the flicker of light counteractively seemed to darken the morning as I began to rotate the mental cylinder of my patterns of emotional infidelities, traces of pride, narrow-minded approaches, lukewarmness, and mountainous uncertainties. I was grateful when the morning's first light filtered into the room as my prompt to leave for work, where I blew out the candle and headed quietly out the front door to my truck. As I pulled from the driveway, it often occurred to me that the pilgrimages into the scorched landscape of my mind were pulling me closer to despair. And yet, outrageously as I think back to those mornings, I chose to stay the course of strip-mining my soul.

In time, I came to realize that I had built the entire edifice of my early-morning prayer on me, not God. I couldn't *see* Him because I was always looking at myself. I finally placed the kaleidoscope aside and worked to become recollected in God's presence. Because my stale patterns of processing and "prayer" had formed grooves of habit in my mind, I often had ruthlessly to fight temptations to enter back into the turbulence of my thoughts. For a long span of time, I worked to train myself to seize an unruly emotion or dead-end image of pain the moment it flickered to life in my mind. As I gained hold of it, I tried immediately to surrender it to His mercy. If that morning Krista had had a bad night, I learned to speak to God with few words, often repeating: *Krista needs you. I need you. Come.*

The tempestuous whirlwind in our marriage had marred my intimacy with God through prayer, so I had to relearn the manner of falling under God's gaze in the prayer I knew as a child, just as I had to relearn the act of walking after my brain surgery. Although I had prayed since my parents taught me at my bedside, strangely, it seemed I had forgotten how to pray. The awareness was alarming because I knew my dryness and feelings of exhaustion were expanding, like rumbling black clouds that push across the sky. In my prayerlessness, I knew the Evil One would become even more unsparing with his work. The symmetry was quite simple: in seeing my nakedness, the tempting serpent would offer stacks of sheet music carrying lyrics of self-pitying thoughts, deserved resentments, and unending reminders of lost spousal entitlements, and ask me to sing. Mostly, though, I knew demons would work at a fever pitch to lead me to emotionally dark places to begin the process of a systematic disintegration of hope. Bearing all this in mind moved me to devote myself fastidiously to relearning the untamed operations of meditative prayer to deepen my relationship with Almighty God, whom I needed in a way I never had before.

At night, I'd prop up my pillows and turn the pages of Saint Teresa of Ávila's *The Interior Castle* and Saint John of the Cross' *Dark Night of the Soul*, books that began to become like ribbons of peace in my soul. It took me some time to understand the strange calculus of their mystical way, but once I began to see that they pulled their thoughts and words from the holy imaginations of their souls, and not their minds, they became lanterns lighting my path farther into their interior life. Their words were raw and unfenced and seemed to far transcend any saint or theologian-written archetypes on the topic of union with God. I had an image of Teresa and John reaching into their chest cavities and holding their hearts before God as pieces of poetry. I imagined the Carmelites they instructed often looked at them saucer-eyed, an admixture of incomprehension, wonderment, and envy.

The secret to their fervency seemed paradoxical to me; their towering intellect and mystical power weren't gained through their raptures, visions, and locutions, but by simply loving God like a small child. It seemed the two Carmelite saints spent the entirety of their lives laying their cheeks up against the warm blaze of Christ's burning Sacred Heart, where, like children, they lay bare the inner workings of their souls with no inhibitions.

I was particularly drawn to Teresa's pilgrimage through her seven delineated chambers of a medieval castle (the forward movement of souls toward ultimate spiritual marriage with God). As I began to read *The Interior Castle*, I imagined myself standing open-mouthed in a grassy field before the cosmic stone-faced medieval castle. Because the isolation and pain in my soul were profound, I mentally found myself wanting to race across the drawbridge and into the sacred warmth of the castle's interior. As I read on, though, I repeatedly saw myself falling from the bridge and into the pus-filled moat, where various serpents and snapping monsters began to maul me. Teresa placed real demands on advancement into the castle, even to gain entrance. As I lay there reading, I felt viscerally demoralized. Full betrothal and spiritual marriage to God required spiritual advancement through her seven sets of mansions, and I knew my grudges, frustrations, and moments of pride stunted any real movement. When I began mentally to gather the obstacles and sins preventing my pilgrimage up the castle stairs, the wide drawbridge in my imagination seemed to have narrowed to a tightrope.

I finished Teresa's book uncomfortably awestruck. The chasm between my place in the moat—where I swam from monsters with despair, tiredness, and lazy love tied to my back—and the seventh chamber of divine union with God was billion-starred galaxies and light years away. Because forward movement through the castle demanded a constant amputation of all worldliness and habits of sin, the thought of the pruning and purification needed in my soul was overwhelming, to the point that I considered raising the surrender flag of acedia before even beginning. But when I considered my place in the dark and lonesome waters, the lengthening drawbridge, and Teresa's grave and growing look of concern from beyond the castle's threshold, I engaged.

If I took the chamber-to-chamber advancement with seriousness, I knew it would pose as great a challenge as anything I'd ever considered taking on. Even though the underwater demons were mostly choked off in the moat, they would still have their place behind each chamber shadow, where they would nimbly readjust their methods to pull me back from any forward movement I'd made through renunciation and small increases in virtue. The real challenge at hand, I knew, was to leave the moat and gain entrance to the castle. To do so, I needed to persevere in loving Krista unburdened of any of my habitual emotional hang-ups. I couldn't enter until I surrendered Krista, the future of our marriage, and her complete healing to God.

When I understood that my massive self-amputation was needed to enter into the castle's embrace, I began to regard Teresa's castle as an image of Christ motioning me to his Cross at Golgotha. To *earn* the castle was to love unconditionally; to begin to crucify my fears of the unknown—with no evidence of Krista's recovery—to his Cross. Although He had *foreknowledge* of what the redemption of His death and Resurrection would bring, He asked me to enjoin and nail my *unknowingness* to His Cross. I began to realize the degree to which I fully surrendered my *unknowing* to His Cross would be part and parcel to my castle advancement. This *forgetting of self* was the life-long secret of Teresa and John—the sacred secret of all of the saints—who didn't just present themselves to Christ at the Cross, but nailed themselves to it.

With a clearer idea of the castle, I set my eyes on the purgative demands the first chamber placed on me. I knew the monsters would work themselves into a frenzy when they sensed in me a determination to shed my habits of emotional infidelity to Krista. I begged God to enter my weak places and to spread seeds for a muscular type of unsparing love for Krista to take root. In the meantime, the Carmelites led me to tether myself to God's gaze through meditative prayer and consistent demonstrations of unrequited spousal love.

Since the earliest days of Krista's drinking, I often recognized how the Evil One modified his approaches with me. If I had managed to reign in and overcome the habit of an unruly emotion, he pulled from his cabinet of wiles to take me down in a different fashion. Aware of his ever-shifting patterns and transmogrifications, I battled him with one weapon more than any other: I set my face like flint and worked repeatedly to surrender everything to God. Krista needed me to love her as a man must, and Satan, I knew, would work inexhaustibly to turn my thoughts inward, where I'd allow loneliness and escalating hopelessness to prompt me effeminately to consider divorce. The Evil One wanted the annihilation of my family. Of course, he would work to disturb Krista and me in different fashions, each particular to our weaknesses and wounds, but I felt back then that he was going to direct a greater portion of his attention into destroying me. The answer to winning the war was gaining entrance into the solitude of the castle. In there, I knew, was enlightenment, order, and the strengthening graces I needed to ward off the coming attacks.

Teresa and John intimately knew the power of Satan, so they were naked in their need for God. Between each line of their poetry, letters, and masterpieces on prayer lay a single idea: to lay one's head against Christ's heart in a mystic marriage. That level of divine intimacy demanded their complete denial of sensory pleasures, consolations, and the allures of the world. The journey to God could only really begin for me when I felt my soul actually burn in similar fashion.

A few of Teresa's words at that time spoke directly to me: *Kevin—Let nothing disturb you, let nothing frighten you, all things are passing away: God never changes. Patience obtains all things; whoever has God lacks nothing; God alone suffices.* Her tender reminder was the handhold she offered for me to cross the drawbridge. As I switched off the light for sleep, my soul had been set right once again for God; tenderized for recollection the following morning.

I'd light the candle on the ledge at around 5 A.M., where I began to sit in silence for about thirty minutes. Whenever my mind strayed into the borderland of distraction, I got into the habit of taming it with a slowly repeated whisper—*Holy Spirit, rest on me.* In the noiselessness, I began to comprehend—*to know* for the first time in a long time—that God was mysteriously at work, as if He were noiselessly moving through dark places in me to bring light. I imagined Him cutting away wrong patterns of thinking with a small carving knife. As I gave way to Him, I spoke in the small words of a child and gently asked Him to replace my soul debris with His love and graces. I repeatedly handed Krista and me to Him as wounded lambs who'd survived the fangs of a wolf, telling Him we'd lost the path and were alone. I thanked Him for finding us and setting us right. But even as my "thank you" left my mouth, I felt agitated by its incongruity. Krista and I were still a moon's distance away from settled peace. Despite myself, and despite my suspicions, I did believe then that He had mysteriously placed Krista and me on His back. It was a warm image—and quite a humbling revelation—to see myself lying like a rag doll right alongside Krista, draped over the saving Shepherd's shoulder.

I was no longer bringing the swallowing sea of my emotions into prayer. Like the pair of Carmelites, I began speaking to God with my heart held in my hand. But because of the intensity of the prayer, I often softened and began to speak to God as a friend. I shared details about the upcoming work day, the latest on the kids, and random thoughts and asked for His blessings. I found that speaking out loud, just above the tone of a whisper, seemed to bring me closer to Him in a way that purely mental prayer couldn't do. If Krista had a bad night, I calmly whispered how it hurt me and was candid about feeling alone. As Jesus befriended the outcasts, poor, and wretchedly pained, I knew His eyes were riveted to me in the poverty of my aloneness. In those moments, I imagined His eyes moistening, regarding me as He did Beloved John as he rested his head against His heart.

In time, the locked doors He had opened led me down a new symmetry of understanding. If I remained obedient to God, I would love Krista without conditions. As

Christ looked upon me and loved me as a frail vessel, I was to do the same for Krista, whom I knew noiselessly screamed for my love from beneath her invisible sea of pain. I simplified my life around a single idea: Everything was a choice between two certain outcomes. Crucified love, devoid of sensible consolations, would bring peace into a disharmonious time. Succumbing to my emotions would be prompts for the Evil One to send demons down to destroy us both.

Thereafter, I knew Beloved John's simple gesture of staying close to Christ's Sacred Heart would be far more efficacious than my years of fasting and penances and unsettling looks through that wretched kaleidoscope of my shortcomings. This small mental adjustment—remaining as close as I could to Jesus' heart—opened up a revolution of newfound peace and direction. Although my plans to "fix" Krista had always seemed to have run aground, I saw that they had actually served to prepare *my own heart* for the work that needed to be done in *me* so I might love Krista as God willed.

Chapter 5

The Hermitage in the Desert

As I began to oblige the purgation of my weaknesses, the drawbridge simultaneously widened. Because the pilgrimage up the castle steps had just begun, I narrowed my habits to those Teresa assured would enable forward movement during the earliest parts of the journey. I recollected my thoughts each morning and asked God to sustain me for any tough moments that might rear up later that day.

At the same time, images of my children swirled in my thoughts throughout the day. Although I found myself continually begging God to guard them, I knew He expected me as their father to make the hard decisions practically and manfully on their behalf. Despite recurring thoughts of the backwardness of my decision of wrapping a code of silence around the ferocious grip of their mom's habits—arguably having left them like gazelles surrounded by crouched lions in tall grasses—I continued to shield them from their mom's habits until I knew they were being impacted by the mysterious weight of it all. They still seemed entirely unaware of Mom's woundedness; at least I hoped so. Even caught in her struggles, Krista fought hard to show her best face to the kids. But they were growing older, and the extrapolations of the ugliness were obvious—so I got on my knees each morning and gave my children over to God, then worked with diligence to increase my time with them. When we were one-on-one, I asked delicately worded questions I thought would reveal the inner workings of their souls, then looked deeply into the nooks and crannies of their eyes.

I began to research articles on "children of alcoholics." Although the effects on them were clearly defined, I could find little to direct me to appropriate parenting methods. Virtually every article strongly encouraged attending Al-Anon meetings, where spouses could share their pain and hear from other pain-stricken souls.

One Saturday morning, I drove to an Al-Anon meeting, where I joined two dozen others. For two hours we sat in a circle of folding chairs where God was never mentioned. I remember sharing with the group, "My own welfare is not my concern; it's how my wife's behaviors will impact my children." A woman from the group instantly corrected me: "You being here has nothing to do with your children; it's about handling your own self-care and equilibrium." Others immediately jumped in to steer me, the newcomer who didn't get it, in the right direction. Fifteen minutes later, I felt like I had just failed the class. I thought one or two others from the group would speak up to commiserate with my feelings, but no one did. I sat with my styrofoam coffee cup, perplexed and lonesome.

Although the Al-Anon group would have ambushed me with wagged fingers and cacophonies of tsk-tsks, my mind kept on the practical matters of my children. If I wasn't a witness of good cheer and paternal care in their presence, then I was a failure as their father and unwittingly raising them in a House of Usher. Although I knew Gabby and Sean could not be kept immune from the deleterious effects of their mom's Jekyll-and-Hyde behaviors for much longer, I worked feverishly to reroute any visible undercurrents of darkness in our home. We ate dinner each night as a family and leisurely discussed our days. Sean and I talked baseball, watched the Orioles each night, and played catch in the back field. I sang goofy songs and took walks with Gabby and Shannon. I attended their sporting events. I prayed with them. We climbed mountains together and did those things that dads do—but I knew the Band-Aid would eventually come off. Shadows were lengthening. Wounds began to appear in the open, and I was at work eleven hours each day. My children needed the maternal care of their mom as much as they needed the paternal care from me.

Krista had prayed a Rosary with us in a slurred voice. She was napping most days. One night, when she saw my text to a friend, a recovering alcoholic, about attending an Al-Anon meeting, she threw my cell phone in our backyard pond. At the beach one weekend, after an attempt to dissuade her from drinking, she drove home without a word. When the kids questioned her abrupt departure, I told them Mom had to tend to the horses at the barn, a partial lie. Krista didn't attend the annual mother-daughter tea at Gabby's school; she was perhaps the only mom to miss. She told me later that night, with teary eyes, that it was just too much pressure. The isolating effects of her habits were pushing her farther back into her cave, where the enemy whispered sweet and duplicitous words that became lodestars pulling her farther back.

The darkest moment for me occurred one summer afternoon after I had invited Krista to sit down with me in the dining room to listen to Mary Chapin Carpenter's version of John Lennon's *Grow Old with Me*. I had heard the song on the radio for the first time earlier in the week outside of a job site. The song of a lover's invitation to grow old with the other pulsed in every line, speaking precisely to the life I desired with Krista. Before the end of the song, I realized I was weeping. I got out of my truck wondering if the foreman noticed my bloodshot eyes. After replaying the song a few times at home, I decided to share it with Krista later in the week, when the timing was right.

One afternoon, I queued it up on my laptop and asked her to sit next to me. I told her I knew that I had failed her over the years in telling her of my love for her. As she silently listened to me, I suddenly felt the part of the high schooler who puts together a mix tape of romantic songs for a girl who didn't want it. I clumsily asked if she would listen to the words of what lay in my heart, words I hoped would move her. Past the midway point of the song, she pushed her chair from the table and left the room, leaving the words of Chapin Carpenter's smoky voice unlistened to:

> Grow old along with me
> Whatever fate decrees
> We will see it through
> Because our love is true
> God bless our love . . .

Despite no evidence that Krista's drinking would one day end, I left the outcome to God and stepped farther with Him into the ugliness of the groan and rejected the customary armament of future Al-Anon meetings, interventions, and medical advice. My lone-man approach would have drawn the scorn of many, but I firmed in my decision to trust God alone as the repairer of Krista's soul. Hope, the oft-overlooked theological virtue, became the bear claw I knew would one day snag and subdue—and eventually kill—the perennial wolf at the door that I knew then was a single thing: the seemingly unkillable demon of shame.

As I moved forward, visits to my uncle's grave held a different resonance. I began to pray with him more peacefully, asking him to intercede to strengthen my resolve and to break up any threats to my family's future. I had gained ground and deepened my faith in Krista's healing, but the brute matter of her isolation and binge drinking too often were speartips that cut me to the core.

Since his murder, numberless folks shared with me my uncle's time-honored response when they approached him with their own agonies: "But where is your trust in God in this?" he'd ask in a booming voice, where he would shake his head and smile as blue Irish eyes flashed hope. He wasn't a priest who proposed Osteen-like solutions; he said only a patient acceptance of the cross would bring peace. Willing saints endured the desert of their crucifixions, he told them, through naked displays of faith and trust that God stood on the other side.

In the lengthening shadows of those early evenings in the cemetery, I imagined him saying the same to me from the silence of his grave, wagging his head and looking into my eyes with intensity. *Kevin, you're earning the path; keep your trust and move forward.* He was leading me to the sacred valleys of the desert saints, who surrendered every comfort to God. Their deserts were dark nights of the soul. When they entered these places of desolation, their seeming forsakenness could only be overcome through an image of Christ, not as an aped-mirage of replenishing water, but as a Savior who within the howling winds carried them in His arms.

During those graveyard visits, an image emerged that I had never considered. I had always regarded myself as the poor beggar at the feet of Christ. But in prayer, it came to me that it was actually Christ who came to me as the beggar. It was He who knocked on the door of my soul, wanting entrance to shine light in my dark night. Within

my marital disconsolation, He as my God, and not my
efforts, was the torchlight.

For the first time, it occurred to me that I was in the
midst of a dark night of the soul in the manner in which
John of the Cross had explained. I began to move practically
to understand how to abide within it. I wanted to know of
individuals over the years who had lived through it.

I began to spend a little less time in meditative prayer
and greater portions of my mornings unhurriedly reading
the stories of the Desert Prophets of the Old Testament.
Starting with Abraham, I moved to Elijah, Ezekiel, Moses,
and even to John the Baptist and Paul. As I began to understand their level of faith during seemingly fatal conditions,
each became like mental icons of sand-whipped wanderers
who had transformed deserts into places of encounter. The
desert wasn't a place for them to subdue and turn around
the dark circumstances and challenges in their lives. It was
a place to go to God naked of everything except trust in
Him. Each grabbed his walking stick and entered the desolation of the wilderness unhesitatingly, knowing God
would speak there, as Moses reminded the desert-bothered
Israelites through poetry: "He found him in a desert land,
and in the howling waste of the wilderness; he encircled
him, he cared for him, he kept him as the apple of his eye"
(Deut 32:10).

The wilderness of aridity and desolation was not a hor-
rible condition in which to flee; it was a crucible of opportunity to walk more deeply into the wastelands to encounter
God. God sent Abraham onto a bleak desert mountain to
sacrifice his only son. After rousing Elijah from his death
wish, God told him to walk for forty days through the
desert and to Mount Horeb and later on a desert road to
Damascus. Moses was sent into the wilderness where revelations and miracles were given during the most dark and
wretched periods. Even Paul was pulled into the desert after

his conversion. And, of course, John the Baptist was forged into prophetic fire there. Aware of the withering conditions John chose as his home, Jesus said of him: "Among those born of women there has arisen no one greater than John" (Mt 11:11).

The Book of Sirach became a torchlight:

My son, if you come forward to serve the Lord,
    remain in justice and in fear,
    and prepare yourself for temptation.
Set your heart right and be steadfast,
    incline your ear, and receive words of understanding,
    and do not be hasty in time of calamity.
Await God's patience, cling to him and do not depart,
    that you may be wise in all your ways.
Accept whatever is brought upon you,
    and endure it in sorrow;
    in changes that humble you be patient.
For gold and silver are tested in the fire,
    and acceptable men in the furnace of humiliation.
Trust in God, and he will help you;
    hope in him, and he will make your ways straight.
Stay in fear of him, and grow old in him.

You who fear the Lord, wait for his mercy;
    and turn not aside, lest you fall.
You who fear the Lord, trust in him,
    and your reward will not fail;
you who fear the Lord, hope for good things,
    for everlasting joy and mercy.
You who fear the Lord, love him,
    and your hearts will be made radiant.
Consider the ancient generations and see:
    who ever trusted in the Lord and was put to shame?
Or who ever persevered in his commandments and was
        forsaken?
    Or who ever called upon him and was overlooked?

For the Lord is compassionate and merciful;
    he forgives sins and saves in time of affliction,
    and he is the shield of all who seek him in truth.
Woe to timid hearts and to slack hands. (Sir 2:1–12)

Even Saint Peter, who lived in perhaps the most withering type of desert—the metaphorical one born in him after his threefold betrayal—poured into my mind like honey. Perhaps the healing of the stain of Peter's memory had to be forged in the desert, where he begged for God to purify his self-hatred and shame:

In this you rejoice, though now for a little while you may have to suffer various trials, so that the genuineness of your faith, more precious than gold which though perishable is tested by fire, may redound to praise and glory and honor at the revelation of Jesus Christ.... And after you have suffered a little while, the God of all grace, who has called you to his eternal glory in Christ, will himself restore, establish, and strengthen you. (1 Pet 1:6–7; 5:10)

Over and over, the stories of these once-desert-purified saints from Scripture pointed me to standing firm in the twofold desert of my dark night and Krista's shame and woundedness. Each awaited God in seeming Hell. My desert, on the other hand, came within the structured opulence of modern American life. The Desert Prophets chose a complete amputation of comforts and withering aloneness to hear God. I was on my own pilgrimage with three square meals, an air-conditioned home, weekly paychecks, the love of my children, and an occasional Orioles game at Camden Yards. My desert, although real, was also allegorical. Within my worldly riches, I knew I wasn't fit to say I was even in the fight for my family—and sustained interior peace—without continuing to strip myself of comforts.

It came to me that the fight for Krista was really an invitation to confront myself interiorly even more deeply. The pulverizing effects of my desert opened up a mysterious space for me to examine the actual level of my trust in God. Within the aridity of its waterlessness, silence, and lack of all emotional consolations, I knew my trust in God *could* act as a wine press if I gave Him all of me. If I surrendered to Him my doubts, I knew He would nourish me with his Blood and make the most remote outposts of my soul places of transformation.

There was one hurdle, though, that I couldn't shake. It was the demon that lived in every desert shadow. It was my doubt in the promise of better days. After paying witness to multiple years of Krista handling her pain in harmful ways, I didn't know how—or, better yet, I didn't trust how—she would come to know order and peace. All I desired then was a single event: Krista's peace. That simple idea streamed relentlessly into my imagination like variegated light from stained glass. In a way, that idea struck me as entrance into the seventh chamber at the top of the castle, but I was still nowhere near it.

To work to overcome that immovable thorn of doubt, I had to continue anchoring myself to the action of trusting like a small child. At heart, the Desert Prophets were like children who *knew* their Father would never lose sight of them, even when He fell cruelly silent or, in Abraham's case, requested he do something unthinkable.

My life, I felt then, hinged on whether I truly trusted God. So I built myself a small hermitage in the quiet valley of my soul and attempted to pay a visit at various points in the day. I began to see that I couldn't step within it until I completely stilled my mind and worked to separate all of my thoughts from everything, desiring total union with God. As I became more self-aware, I set up mechanisms to detach from everything except God. When I managed to accomplish it, I was able to enter the quiet hermitage and found that God instantly quieted my heart. With that intimacy with God, I became like the sleepy-eyed child on a winter night cozy beneath his blankets.

In that still place in my soul, my wandering Irish imagination often had me in a tall lighthouse whose thin beam of light shone into the darkness of an unsettled sea. I was standing on a wind-rattled catwalk next to what felt like the invisible presence of God. I looked into night fires scattered along the coastline and watched the spinning blaze of light search out distressed mariners. It felt so good standing noiselessly next to this muscular presence, where I imagined God wearing a secret smile.

In time, I saw that Krista wasn't on His mind in the way in which she was on mine. It was me. *He knew*: Even in this place of my emergence—in this warm desert hermitage—I carried monstrous scabs of resentment with me into the desert.

Tongue-tied, I spit out, *Lord, I am a great sinner. Help me.*

The dark memories to which I clung suffocated full trust in God. It was partially *me* who restrained Krista's healing. Although I had surrendered her to His providence, I hadn't surrendered *myself* without traces of self-pity and bitterness. By my own hand, I had carved scarring, indelible memories into myself.

God spoke words that hit me in the heart.

Krista lives in the sea—but don't you dare judge her by the wreckage she clings to.

Don't take your eyes off of her. Remember how you first loved her. Now—love her more.

Chapter 6

Light Blinks On

One night Krista broke her wrist falling out of the bathtub, a seemingly dismal accident that set in motion a series of events that, although it would take time, ultimately turned back tides of disorder.

A week following the surgery needed to re-set her wrist, Krista and I attended a half-day retreat sponsored by the Monsignor Thomas Wells Society, where a few hundred folks gathered on a cool autumn morning as four priests shared memories of my deceased uncle and presented talks on growth in the spiritual life. Each priest and many attendees were close to my uncle, so it seemed as if he could be in the room with us that day.

Then I felt his presence among us when I saw Father Dan Leary step through a side door of a hall.

Without premeditation, a thought came unbidden from thin air, as if a guardian angel or an inspiration from my uncle placed it there. *Have Father Dan pray over Krista's soul . . . use her wrist.*

Unconsciously, I stopped midway through a conversation with a retreatant and approached Krista, who had been standing behind a line of tables and with her unbroken hand had been handing out Chick-fil-A boxed lunches. I asked if she would come with me. I wanted her to meet someone.

Father Leary and I had become close friends over the years. He was the same priest with whom I shared my grief in the Jamaican jungle just a few months prior to this accident in 2016. Well-known as a retreat master, for magnanimous work as a pastor, and his Masses of Anointing, he had established a commanding presence throughout the Archdiocese of Washington. Many folks claimed illnesses had either softened or been completely healed after being prayed over by him. He was scheduled to present his talk following lunch.

"Krista, there's a priest here I think you would really like," I said. "He's a good priest and he's got a great sense of humor." Krista's eyes squinted. "I'm still handing out lunches," she said. "I can't now." Months earlier, she had rejected Father Flum at our front door. Although I was no longer suffering the effects of the doghouse, Krista was leery of coming close to any priest.

A long-time friend of mine stood nearby. "Becky to the rescue! Will you do Krista and me a favor and hand out the rest of the lunches?" I asked. "Just thirty or more to go." Becky instantly jumped in.

Krista haltingly smiled and thanked the volunteer, and I began to pray. As she walked to me from behind the table, her smile vanished, unhappy with what she perceived as a possible mini-intervention.

At that moment, from across the hall, Father Leary and I made eye contact. He saw that Krista was at my side. He broke away from a conversation with folks who had greeted him at the door. He approached us.

Father Leary had become arguably the hardest-working priest in the diocese. After four years at Villanova University, the former college fraternity president experienced a radical conversion shortly after graduation that led him to attend as many as three weekday Masses a day. When he entered Mount Saint Mary's Seminary in Emmitsburg, Maryland, in 1992, he had turned his life over to God. But he hadn't parted with his pranking college humor. In 2011, the first words he spoke to me were, "Hey, Wells, that book you wrote has been great," he said. "I use it all the time whenever I run out of toilet paper." Our friendship became firm that day. He stepped in front of me and extended his hand. When I went to shake it, he quickly shifted it and extended it to Krista. "Great to meet you, Krista," he said. "I'd much rather shake your hand than touch his dirty paw." Krista smiled and softly said hello. Sensing her unease, Father Leary turned to me.

"Thanks for taking the time to make it out here, Father Dan," I said, leaning into the banter. "We put you third in the lineup of speakers because no one ever listens to the guy who speaks after lunch."

"Wells, get me a sandwich," he commanded, laughing.

"That's another thing, Father," I replied. "We made a decision not to serve you any food."

"Wells, I don't want any of your food, and I can't eat anyway. I've been fasting for your soul," he quickly responded. "Now stop talking to me and let me talk to your wife."

"Krista, meet Father Dan. Do your best not to listen to anything he says today," I lightheartedly advised. "In fact, why don't we skip his talk and eat some more chicken sandwiches."

"Your husband's a loser. You shouldn't have married him," Father Leary said over the noise of the crammed church hall. "Krista, let's pray he gets better."

Krita was enjoying the back-and-forth when I gently reached for her arm. I slowly lifted it from her side and showed Father Leary the soft cast covering her forearm. I explained that Krista was still in pain after breaking her

wrist and asked if he would pray over it. Amid the lunchtime commotion of conversations, laughter, and drag of
metal chairs, Father Leary softly reached for her arm and
looked with tenderness into her eyes. Rattled by his sudden change in demeanor, a burst of obvious discomfort
covered her. She looked to the floor.

"Krista, would you like me to pray over your wrist?" he
asked. With her eyes still fixed to the ground, Krista nodded her head. The noise all around seemed to soften as an
oceanic weight lifted. Sixteen years had passed since she had
allowed herself to become vulnerable before a priest, when
two nights before his murder, my uncle spoke to her tired
soul about her childlessness and the mystery of the Cross.

"Let's go outside where there's not so much noise,"
Father Leary said. "We can pray there."

They walked toward a side door that led to a basketball
court I played on as a small child. As they moved through
the crowd, it seemed the Red Sea had parted. When they
stepped into the area ahead and disappeared from sight,
my tears welled and I thanked my uncle for activating
what seemed a true grace. The fractured wrist, I knew,
would go unacknowledged within the sudden movement
of spiritual subterfuge. Father Leary's whispered prayers
were meant to pull back heaven's curtain and unveil God's
shocking light to a travailed soul. I imagine the Holy Spirit
on that sunny day outside of low-ceilinged Whitemarsh
Hall rushed like a waterfall into an empty basin, disturbing
what seemed to me then her unruly chorus of demons.
But I also understood that grace, as it perfected nature,
would take time. Still, I knew his prayers would mark the
prelude to a drawn-out rescue mission, when seeming
demons, one by one, would begin to flee.

Years later, when recalling this moment in time, Krista
remarked, "When he began to pray, I felt the warmth of

God for the first time in years. But even then, I fought as hard as I could against it. I didn't know how to live without what I was doing to myself."

Later that night, Krista didn't mention a word about what I sensed had set in motion the invisible movement of sanctification and healing. Her deathly silence stretched into the week that followed; I supposed that she viewed my abrupt introduction to Father Leary as another sneak attack, reminiscent of the one months earlier on the ruinous evening Father Flum knocked on our door. She built a wall of ice around her, and rather than trying to break through, I, too, kept quiet. I knew any probing would stoke the embers of her defiance and add to her layers of anger for me. A wordless stalemate about Father Leary's prayers began.

Still, within the cave of Krista's secret silence, I knew she had been pierced. Father Leary had reached past the scabs of her woundedness and touched her soul through something supernatural and raw. I knew it simply because I saw a certain uneasy peace permeate a small part of her for the first time in years. She smiled more and seemed lighter. It was her first small taste of the joy of renewal and inner peace.

Early one Saturday morning, as Krista headed out the door, she surprisingly informed me that she was driving out to meet with Father Leary at his parish, Saint Andrew the Apostle. Outwardly, I remained composed. "That's great. He's a good priest." I said nothing else, nor did she. The kids were still asleep. As she pulled her car from the driveway, I knelt and prayed to God to equip Father Leary with the wisdom that would begin to recapture the peace that alcohol and wounds had strip-mined from her soul.

When she returned home, she discussed very little of the visit. She had built a fortress around her innermost life.

Still, Father Leary's prayers over Krista's wrist marked an inflection point in her life: She had become vulnerable to receiving the words, care, and anointing of a priest.

In the following month, Krista met twice more with Father Leary. She remained aloof about her visits, only mentioning their conversations in broad terms, but because Father Leary had become a close friend, I was convinced the Spirit was likely moving in her. I knew him well, so I also knew he was addressing her woundedness some-how. He had established some renown as a connoisseur of pinpointing long-held wounds and pulling them out to set free long-suffering souls. Meanwhile, Krista's habits stayed firm. She continued to drink in private with impunity.

One day in 2017, Krista told me Father Leary had invited her to attend a mission trip to Jamaica, the same one I had attended the previous year. Krista would be asked to do one thing there: to love the severely developmentally and physically disabled children and adults. But I knew Krista, not the community, would be overpowered by their saint-like purity and guilelessness. I just knew her gentle heart would be captured by those she was going to serve.

Days before her departure, Krista shared her fear. "I don't know anyone on the trip. And I've never done any-thing like this. I don't know if I can go."

"The people in the community need your quiet way of love, Krista. They'll be drawn to you," I said. "Your doubts are from the devil. He wants to keep you away." I wondered then if her doubts stemmed from the realization that she would be spending a week without wine.

"Kevin, there are others who've done this already. I have no idea what I'm doing," she said, her eyes moisten-ing. Many of the residents had rare skeletal and limb abnor-malities that confined them to cribs. Others suffered from severe autistic and severe developmental disorders. "The other people going will know how to care for them," she said. "To be honest, I'm scared to go."

"I was afraid when I went, too," I encouraged. "But when the gate swings open to this place, it all melts away. And when you walk down the hill and into their community for the first time, you'll feel like you're entering what appears to be a kingdom of forgotten saints. That's when the uneasiness left me. All they want is your love."

Krista sent me a text on her first day in the Jamaican jungles: "I saw a sign above a door that said, 'Surrender,'" she wrote. "I think I can do this." She couldn't have known the fashion in which I read her text. I had spent the week fasting and praying that a resident's tender glance, too-tight hug, or act of unpretentious love would spring an implosion of graces and ignite the change that would turn her from her dependence on wine.

She couldn't surrender it, though. At home, after a bursting out of first fervor, her pattern of drinking returned, and the distance between us resumed. Something, though, I knew, had penetrated her. Although she mostly kept quiet about the mission trip and stayed secretive about what serving the community had opened up in her, she glowed when speaking about the Jamaicans. From the onset, they had lavished her with unpretentious and childlike love, tender gestures that pierced Krista's heart. So it was there she went—to the euphoria of serving the poorest of the poor.

In the two years that followed, Krista began recruiting and leading mission trips to the Jamaican community of disabled children and adults. In a way, though, it had become another addiction. All these years later, Krista told me she needed the high of finally feeling good about herself.

Always, though, after returning from the high of the mission trip, she boomeranged back to the secrecy of her ways. These were the darkest times, when Satan's work was masterful. In Krista, he had an afflicted soul—and with great ease, he plunged his talons into her thinking, maneuvering her to an embrace of her own benevolence and care that she lavished on the least of these. Overnight, it seemed, notions of her own altruism poured in, nourishing her with poisoned manna. Feelings of self-worth overpowered the reality that the escalation of her dark habits might soon cause the ruination of our family.

Satan was still in the saddle then, and his machinations seemed magisterial. He'd managed to sweep Krista into his darkest countryside; she'd been granted safe passage into his kingdom of pride and self-importance. In the simmering, lie-scorched landscape, her runaway shame vanished in a puff of smoke. Fenced into this land, a soul-damning vainglory emerged, where it began to grow in scope and velocity.

Despite the fresh corrosive wrinkle set into the spiritual war, I sensed in God's providence that He was trying to orchestrate something powerful in me. He wanted total surrender of Krista to Himself; long-game work, where slowly but surely my endurance and faith in His providence would bring about healing.

I knew without question that Krista had encountered the light of Christ in the souls of the Mustard Seed Community, where a scattering of sacred seeds had been planted deeply, but as yet had been unnoticed by her. It seemed inevitable that the harvest would finally come when her habits fully came to light. They would be made manifest when Krista saw her brokenness reflected in the eyes of a population of disabled and mostly helpless souls. In them, she would recognize the radiance and joy of the lived cross. And when she grasped and accepted her own disability in the midst of theirs, she would perceive only layers and layers of cynicism and regret. This community and Christ's presence within it would be great instructors of the soul. My hope was that the pure lives lived by its residents would act to peel away years of decay. As the disabled community pined for Krista's gentle touch, she would begin to pine for the safe furnace of God's Sacred Heart—where she might become vulnerable enough to allow Christ to burn away years of devastation and deceit, opening a fresh land where logic, reason, and good fruit prevailed.

It would take time though. She stopped visiting Father Leary once he began to address her addiction to drink.

When a few of the mission trips went poorly, she brought home a disturbed heart, where she laid bare an agglomeration of resentments and frustrations, some of which were justified. And the demons, of course—it always seemed to me—were right on time with their wheedling words: *The mission went wrong because of X. You were the lone star.* And so began the chase for the perfect mission trip, perfect chaplain, and perfect set of missionaries. All was set in motion—where, of course, expectations were never met.

When Krista arrived home, her drinking and isolation resumed.

It was during this dry time that a phenomenon began to occur. In the evenings, when I stepped out of the house for an errand, attended a men's group, or watched one of Gabby or Sean's games, I could *feel* Krista was drinking. I could have been watching Gabby run down a field with her field hockey stick when a spontaneous feeling of melancholy, and even dread, would suddenly and parasitically cover me. I *knew* she was drinking at that moment. Inevitably, when I returned home, Krista had either gone off to bed or refused to make eye contact, her eyes bleary with drink. She knew that I knew, and she was too helpless to care.

I remember within this dark night of the soul always sweeping floors then. I would call it a habit, but it had really become more like a consoling addiction or tic that mysteriously softened the crisis unfolding in my home. Before work, with everyone asleep and the coffee brewing in the darkness of the kitchen, I would go to the laundry room, grab the broom and begin to sweep the hardwood floors in the family room, living room, hallways, and lastly, kitchen, before pouring myself a thermos of coffee and heading to work.

The habit began after a priest friend, a chaplain who had prayed with and celebrated hundreds of Masses for soldiers in war zones, told me a story of the ancient port city of Ephesus following Christ's Ascension into Heaven. In his years of research on the city on the Aegean Sea, he discovered Ephesus was populated with retired Roman centurions who may have received word about the resurrected Christ from one of their own—the converted centurion who marveled at the foot of the Cross. His story became the story of Ephesus—and, all of a sudden, what once was known as an ordered seaside town tucked in a valley became perhaps the most Christ-centered and -ordered city in the world.

My priest friend told me that at the time of Christ's crucifixion, retired centurions were awarded large plots of land that overlooked the sea and sun-splashed mountains as a reward for their service to the Roman emperor Tiberius. The Mediterranean climate and fertile soil produced abundant fields of raisins, figs, grapes, wheat, and vegetables. A short walk to the coastline brought back a garden of fruit from the sea. Boar roaming the hillsides made for easy sport and dinner feasts. Drawing from their training, discipline, and military planning, the soldiers' families, homes, and fields boasted a solidity and unmovable grace.

In his Letter to the community, Paul commended the families of Ephesus for their great fraternal love: "For this reason, because I have heard of your faith in the Lord Jesus and your love toward all the saints, I do not cease to give thanks for you" (Eph 1:15–16). Considering the orderliness of their lives and what they had received through Christ, the Ephesians were regarded by Paul as inhabitants of a land of folks striving to be saints. When Our Lady and Beloved John eventually settled there, Ephesus caught fire.

"Kevin, these soldiers were disciplined before they knew Christ," he said. "Then Christ enters their hearts and everything changes. Hearing the stories from Jesus' mother and His beloved apostle, Ephesus becomes a place of great harmony. Children play carefree in the fields, the men become sacrificial, humble, and life-giving to their wives. And the wives—they feel safe and loved. Their husbands are no longer fighting wars, and these women become the backbone of Ephesus. They keep everything upright and ordered.

"They pass on the stories of Jesus to their children. Their homes are clean. Porches are broom-swept. It is a city bathed in bliss. Everything has order."

Thereafter, Ephesus became an icon burned deep into my soul. I swept and prayed: *Lord, help us. Give my family this type of order.* After many attempts to bring order to disorder, I knew there was little I could do to change the circumstances, so I adjusted my perspective, swept, and loved Krista as best as I was able.

Then, one day, out of the clear blue, Krista told me she was considering attending a silent weekend retreat. She had never attended a retreat alone in her life. She shared her jitters with me. Although her drinking pattern and behaviors remained on a steady course, the commingling of Father Leary's direction and witness of the pure souls in

Jamaica had pierced and opened something new in her, or put a different way, a few pieces of her armor had somehow suddenly fallen away. Her conversion would be a drawn-out one and come in stages and degrees, like the blind man who saw humans walking as trees before Jesus laid hands on him again and he could see clearly.

The women's retreat was two months away. I held my breath and prayed for what seemed that long. I knew her inspiration would twist and be blown into the four winds each one of those sixty days, and demons, I imagined, would work with relentlessness to mock and annihilate Krista's desire.

Pre-dawn sweeping intensified.

The Friday morning of the retreat weekend arrived. Krista packed a weekend bag and took off for the same retreat house three generations of my family had attended. Since college, I had spent a winter weekend at the old Jesuit retreat house buried in the thick of a forest, bordering gentle southern Maryland farmland. The sprawling maroon-brick estate rests footsteps from a steep cliff that overlooks a broad expanse of the Potomac River, where a tribe of Indians settled and held the land sacred centuries earlier. You would be hard-pressed to find more tranquil and striking acreage on the eastern seaboard of America. Sunsets there make tough men cry. On these 250 acres, bald eagles soar, shooting stars fall, and a covering of silence falls like snow into wearied souls, to allow space for God to be heard.

A text came in that evening, at about 9:45 P.M.

Things are going well. The last talk just ended. I'm going to confession. Two priests are here. One is Father Matt Fish.

The other is a priest named Father Flum. Do you know him?

Krista told me later my response came back in all caps, spaced in two lines:

GO TO FATHER FLUM.
GO FACE TO FACE.

Krista didn't know that night that I was telling her to confess her sins and to look into the face of the priest on whom she slammed the door.

Chapter 7

The Meeting

Krista described stepping into the confessional where she saw a heavy-bearded priest whose head was bowed, seemingly lost in prayer. His eyes were closed; hands gently lay on his lap. The faded purple stole around his neck was plain and narrow; its fabric appeared worn. There was neither gold piping nor fringe. He wore a cassock.

She closed the door and sat down, directly across from him, where she was greeted with noiselessness. He stayed in his monk-like posture, offering her only the silence of his prayer. After a few moments of gathering her courage and wits, she began to unburden herself.

"Bless me, Father, for I have sinned..."

As she began the swim through her soul to lay bare her sins, she didn't expose her drinking.

When she requested absolution, Father Flum raised his head and made eye contact for the first time. Neither, it seemed, recognized the other. He then began to speak to her and delicately propose countermeasures to the habits of her sin. He began to probe more deeply some of the wounds, where a short exchange arose. At some point in the back-and-forth, Krista mentioned my name.

Father Flum paused. He slowly straightened in his chair, and his eyes widened behind his wire-rimmed glasses. His beard may have shaken some. The following exchange is what Krista recalls these years later: "You. You're the one," he said, eyes flashing. "You're the one who wouldn't let me in." He jabbed his index finger at her. "I drove all the way out to your house and you closed your door on me."

Krista was thrown off. She had no idea what the priest was accusing her of; she had completely blotted the night from her memory.

By the look in her eyes, Father Flum instantly discerned she had no remembrance of the night.

Krista shared that he said this: "Well, one night last winter I knocked on your door for a dinner your husband had arranged and you wouldn't let me in," he said. His voice was soft. "Your husband forgot about the date; he was out of town—and you and I spoke at your doorstep. I would say it didn't go very well. And you wouldn't let me in."

In an instant, the light switched on. Krista's face reddened with mortification. A locomotive of memories from the night came back. "Oh, no, I remember," she said, as she recalled the meanness and her mental state that night. "I am sorry. That was a terrible thing I did. I am embarrassed now."

"And I was hungry that night, too. I hadn't eaten a thing all day," Father Flum said in a loud tone that Krista believed others behind her in line could hear. He played it all up and shook his head, thrusting his index finger at her again, into the open space between them. Krista didn't know if the priest was genuinely still angry at her rudeness or if he was having some fun at her expense—or a combination of both.

He saw the wave of discomfort covering Krista, so he changed course and offered her a warm smile indicating he wasn't upset in the slightest degree. When she saw that the priest was at peace with the night, she began to relax as the tense atmosphere in the small confessional faded.

After some time, a sheet of solemnity fell into the confessional again. He settled quickly back into the native strength of his priesthood and returned to his monk-like posture, as if the previous few minutes had never happened. With eyes closed and head fixed to the ground, he fixed his mind back on her soul and began the sacred utterances of absolution.

Before Krista could reach for the doorknob to leave, he asked her quietly, "Would you like to continue this conversation tomorrow?"

"Yes, Father," Krista whispered. "That would be nice."

The following afternoon they met in a room in the basement of the retreat home that overlooked the Potomac River. It was autumn and the towering trees by the cliffside bore striking colors. Father Flum in his cassock sat across from Krista and began gently to ask questions about her life, never again mentioning the event at the doorstep. Krista kept guarded. She did not share her drinking patterns or distance from me. She began to speak about the wounds of her past and the manner in which they had hardened her. She shared feelings of being unloved and isolated. She said she felt a great distance from God and that she had never regarded Him as a truly loving Father.

Father Flum listened intently. After some time, he began to reveal to Krista the immensity of God's love, which broke open dams of new awareness in her.

"God has known you from the beginning of time. Before creating the world, He loved you, Krista," he said. "As you were being formed in your mom's womb, He knew everything about you and of what you would become. And He loved everything He saw. The most beautiful words cannot explain how great His love for you was as His daughter.

"But He also knew how you would suffer in life. As your Father, he saw times that you would be lonely and feel badly hurt, and He suffered with you as you suffered. But Krista, God didn't abandon you at your worst points. As you suffered, He was right beside you. Because you felt pain, He also felt it."

Krista began to cry at the awakening she felt in her heart. After some time, she shared her persistent feelings of isolation and fear. Then she shared her drinking. Father Flum looked into her eyes and stayed quiet as she cried. After some time, he led her into a tender crash course on intimacy with the Eternal God as a loving Father. He said God would become a dominant force of love in her life only when she began to open herself to Him as His needful daughter. The core of anyone's crisis, he said, was a rejection of intimacy and friendship with the Father. As your Father, he told Krista, His only desire was that she would come and abide in Him.

He began to point her back to the method of encountering the Father's eternal embrace.

"When you meet God in prayer, you place yourself in a position to receive a Father's love," he told her. "What God wants is oneness with you, the daughter he's cherished since time began." However, he softly warned her, until she accepted and came to embrace the reality that there was a Father in Heaven looking at her with love, no true intimacy or encounter with Him could take place. He said one would always remain adrift without a true understanding of the Father's love. As Father Flum spoke, Krista remembered, for the first time, wanting to draw closer to God as His wounded daughter.

As they finished up, Father Flum asked Krista if she had an interest in continuing to meet, to which Krista agreed. This was the start of everything; the relationship that would eventually serve to break and save her began that day. Though it would be tested many times, Krista began to hunger for the invigorating feeling of springtime in her soul, but the wild bird within her was still untamed, and wintertime covered too much of her antagonized heart. She wanted the Father-God who desired and loved her, but the tomb she had lived in for so long was familiar and kept calling her back.

The maddening pattern became etched in stone: In the aftermath of a meeting with Father Flum, Krista became like a butterfly fresh out of the cocoon, where her soul presented itself as beautiful and unencumbered. My children and I saw her inner flight, and it brought us great joy. But always, usually a week or two later, like Icarus, she lost her wings and fell. The chain from her tomb kept whiplashing her back.

Month followed month, until one day—*poof*—she wanted to stop seeing Father Flum temporarily. Repeatedly confessing the sin of secret drinking had sickened and shamed and gotten the best of her, despite Father Flum's seeming patience. Although the priest spoke to her soul in spiritual direction as no one ever had, she told him she would not be returning for a while. And with that, Krista returned to the dark place of shame in her tomb. It seemed to me then nothing short of catastrophic.

Her drinking seemed to have become spiritual arsenic poured into my own bloodstream, where it eviscerated the few secret gardens of hope that had grown since she began to see Father Flum regularly. As disbelief in Krista's sudden reversion covered me, I felt pulled into her same valley of aloneness. My faith in God, and the methods of hope to which Teresa, John of the Cross, and the Desert

Prophets led me were vanishing. The realization startled me, because in the gloom of those days, faith in God and Father Flum was all I had.

And, of course, the inevitable came. My two oldest children began to come to see clearly that Mom was unwell. Awareness shone in them; it was the look of children of the Irish Potato Famine, whose eyes searched their father to answer their hunger. And all he could do was look away into fields of decay, but looking away wouldn't do.

One early morning in the office, I shared what had become an existential crisis with my older brother, Dan, finally revealing the long devastation barnacled to my marriage. I told him I needed to reevaluate everything in my life, including my livelihood, where I had served alongside him for seventeen years in the family business.

I told Dan that at the beginning of 2018, I would be leaving work. Due to the grave matter, we agreed to term my departure as "a writing sabbatical"—which it had to become. I needed a job as I stayed home and worked to keep watch over Krista and my family. So, a new life began. Krista seemed to appreciate that I was taking a break from contracting work to write from out of the home, but that sadly didn't change the course of anything.

Chapter 8

Home and Far Afield

To live in accord with the family safeguarding project also required that I actually stay busy writing.

It had occurred to me many times over the past six or seven years to write to priests, many of whom I sensed seemed to be losing their identities as faithful guardians of souls. The power of the priest's anointed hands became clear to me on that dead-end night in the neuro-ICU room when my uncle and Father Stack collaborated to bring God's healing hand down to turn things around. To me, then, there seemed no doubt: no one on earth held more eternal significance than the Roman Catholic priest who unflinchingly embraced the burden of his identity as the slaughtered lamb. *In persona Christi*, holy priests had a certain authority no one else did. Intimately, I felt Father Stack and my uncle raised a dead man back to life.

Over and over, at Sunday and weekday Masses at the parish down the street, I sensed an unwillingness of those priests to accept their crucified state in life. Rather than building for their flock—*and Krista and me*—a bridge that would take us to Heaven, their prophetic voice was damned up in homilies that never introduced conversion of soul, the blood-and-guts pursuit of virtue, and small, self-imposed deaths to self. Selfishly, it was my hope a priest's sermon would produce a transcendent thought or piercing image that would constellate and mysteriously cohere with the movements in Krista's soul. Pitifully, looking back on those days, I remember reading the upcoming Sunday Gospel and considering how Jesus' words might spring conversion in her. I found myself on Sunday mornings internally begging God to put a spectacularly providential sermon onto Father's lips; bending my ear for Father's words on the demoniac in the tombs, the prostitutes, Saul, and the afflicted—and how they gained Heaven through full-on movement to Christ through a converted life—but they never came. In fact, nothing came remotely close to speaking to the depths of Krista's trial from that pulpit. At this sitting, I cannot recall a time when the wages of repeated sin and Hell were mentioned in a homily. The Sacrament of Confession was rarely encouraged. Our Lady, Saint Joseph, Teresa of Ávila, and John of the Cross, tales of the martyrs, the weight of mortal sin, and so forth, were hardly mentioned. Pitifully, I often felt a creeping darkness come into me at Mass and felt myself being pulled back into the pus of Teresa's moat.

Occasionally, during my ten-plus years at the parish, I set up meetings with priests to express my thoughts, but I was often met in the flatlands of faraway stares and nods. These priests heard the zeal behind my pleas, but they certainly could not know my subliminal cry for Krista—*I am begging you for a priesthood of muscularity and sheer fatherly magnanimity*. I often left those meetings feeling judgmental, even hopeless. These priests were not human talismans, I knew. My situation wasn't theirs to repair magically. My expectations of them were unfair; I was just searching for their help along the way.

Krista *wanted* freedom. And I knew, because of her love for holy priests, she now *wanted* a rugged and enduring one—one she would see as willing to climb far down the scaffold into her shame and work to heal her with fatherly wisdom, firmness, and pious care. She needed my uncle Tommy again, one who would look in the eye as he did that last night, when a few nights before his murder, he looked into eyes racked with pain and said—with tears welling in his own eyes—"I'll be there for you throughout it all." That gaze of love and simple promise cracked her wide open. It changed the course of a marriage that was spinning toward ruin. I imagine Christ looked at Mary Magdalen the same way, where his gaze acted as a sort of exorcism that chased away demons of lust. My uncle's look of love had seemingly done the same in redirecting Krista's ferocity to have a baby through IVF into a place of surrender to God. Although I viscerally felt the unfairness of laying my burdens at the feet of priests to fix, I held on to the images of the gazes of Jesus to the prostitute and Tommy to Krista. Those gazes and promises of fatherly love transformed two lives, and—fairly or unfairly—I felt that same fatherly gaze could do the same to exorcise Krista's demons of shame and secret drinking.

She wanted and needed Father Flum again. She reached out to him and apologized for her time away. Father Flum was warmly invited back to meet regularly again. Peace pervaded both of our souls.

My time at home gave me the opportunity to be in Krista's presence for most of the day, where we became closer, even as her healing was still steep mountain-and-valley climbs away. Inch by inch, though, we began climbing, and I had never felt closer to her. We often attended weekday Mass in the early morning and returned home to fall into the patterns of the day. Krista would spend some of her time at the barn with her horse, run errands, and engage in household chores and school pick-ups. I would usually be in my office, writing and researching some of the great priest-saints—Vianney, Bosco, Neri, Kolbe, and others. We'd often have lunch together. Life, alas, had order. It mostly seemed joy-filled and healthy. Until night came, when a splitting apart slowly reemerged.

The lightness and freedom of the Mustard Seed Community and the solidity and fatherly care from Father Flum cast rays of light in her. It was unspoken, but she understood I had *come home* for her and would not move from her side until, in a sense, she was well. All that remained, Krista knew, was for her to look in a mirror and say—*no more*. Gabby was a junior in high school, Sean was a sophomore, and Shannon was a fifth-grader. For the first time, I was seeing them off in the morning and occasionally picking them up from school. I began to teach a class at Sean's school to spend more time with him.

Meantime, my pursuit of comprehending priestly sanctity had set me on what felt like a pilgrimage. These priest-saints from years gone by had escorted me into a graced countryside of heroism, where, one by one, they lined up in formation, a cadre of willing martyrs inflamed with love for Christ and their flocks. For millennia, prior to the advent of Alcoholics Anonymous, recovery programs, and rehabilitation centers, it was often the witness and work of hard-working, zealous priests who helped to separate afflicted souls from their wounds, disordered attachments, and addictions. My study of their lives revealed the reason behind the stunning results of their saving hands: they had made identification with the crucified Christ the centerpiece of their lives. It was there, in union with the Slaughtered Lamb, that a priest found his vocation's tenderest fruit. His willingness to suffer rejection, long hours of unseen prayer and service, and a life set apart produced an infusion of graces for his flock. Kolbe accepted death in a starvation chamber, but Vianney lived in a splintered, claustrophobic confessional. Damien the Leper loved lepers so much that he became one. On and on these priest-saints walked me down the lone path of accompanying Krista. It was when they made victims of themselves that they most resembled Divinity hanging from a cross. Whether it was losing their head as a witness for Holy Mother Church or giving themselves over as a sacrificial expiation to pour love into their flock, each priest integrated and accepted martyrdom in some form into his life. By consenting to daily self-denial, they guarded and sanctified the souls of their parishioners. As they suffered quietly, mortified themselves bodily, and immersed themselves in prayer and Scripture, they drew down God's sanctifying graces. They never ceded ground, and when they were tempted, they prayed themselves through it. These priests seemed to me then like sacred princes, instructing reminders of what God had already set into me—*Crucify your emotions. Love Krista well, and she will swim back.*

I had written a number of chapters and sent them off to eight or nine Catholic publishers. Within a few months, each publisher rejected the book idea. It seemed they collectively did not take to the idea of a member of the laity proposing to priests "how to be a priest." I responded to some of the editors that my book's intent was a simple "plea for apostolic heroism," not to serve as a "how-to manual." But at that point, it didn't matter what I said. It was discouraging news on multiple fronts. I had invested a large amount of time reading, studying, and writing what I thought would be an encouraging spiritual boost to both clergy and laity. I had also interviewed a few dozen members of the clergy, exorcists, seminary rectors, formators, and members of the laity who were heartened by the idea of a heartfelt Catholic man penning an aspirational book for priests. With a suddenly unsunny outlook on the book, I found myself with a dilemma: Do I return to work and waste what progress was being made in Krista and our home, or remain for a while longer to be close to my family? I had given myself a small window of time, and I didn't want to lose my chance to do whatever I could to keep in step with whatever God was calling me to do on horizontal and vertical plains. Horizontally, it was my duty to enter Krista's wound, to love her within it, and to do what I could to bring Christ in to reverse the patterns of thinking. Vertically, my marital vow called me to God through the desert of Krista's spiritual infirmary and to root myself in the fight to lead her to Heaven.

Shortly after the rejections of my book proposal, I was asked, twice on the same day, to contact Monsignor John Esseff, a then ninety-two-year-old mystic regarded by thousands of Catholics and many hundreds of priests as one of the holiest and wisest men in the world. I didn't know him, but after meeting him, he alone became the reason I would continue to write and complete my seemingly orphaned book.

In preparing for my meeting and interview with him, I learned that Monsignor Esseff had spent half of his life exorcising demons. I discovered that likely no priest in the world had spent more time with as many bishops, priests, and seminarians this past century than he had. In 1959, he shared a two-hour conversation in Italy with a *bi-located* Padre Pio. Later in life, he became one of Mother Teresa's closest friends, traveling by her side as her confessor throughout impoverished areas overseas.

But it was his work countering demons that most held my attention, as I thought of Krista. I asked if she'd want to drive with me to Scranton, Pennsylvania, to meet with this uncommon priest. When I told her the story behind the bi-location, she was excited to take the four-hour trip.

As Monsignor Esseff welcomed us into his meager living quarters, he began to relate some of the remarkable stories from his life, his time with Mother Teresa, growing up with a holy family, and of course the bi-location from Padre Pio. After some time, he turned his attention to my book—and the mood of the room took a turn. The warmth and courtesy of his gentle voice departed as his thoughts traveled back into what seemed a malevolent shadow of memories. He began to speak of a heartbreaking landscape of malfeasance, omissions, and seeming dethronement of Catholic teaching to which he had been exposed in American seminaries shortly after he had left holy Mother Teresa's side. It was a time, he said, when darkness was palpable within these institutions. He then proceeded to walk us through a timeline of unholy land mines, describing the lack of discipline, the immaturity, and the homosexual strain he had witnessed in seminaries. He told us he had stopped visiting the majority of them long ago. He told me, "Kevin, those seminarians—so many of them are today's priests. I am going to urge you to continue writing your book. You tell them, as a lamb, you need them to be a shepherd willing to die for you. Tell them you need a priest with a father's heart, not a bachelor who doesn't pray. A priest must be a father who shepherds souls to Heaven. A priest must be Jesus, who dies."

Monsignor Esseff then told us that he wanted to celebrate the Holy Sacrifice of the Mass for us. This Mass seemed of a different order, as if an apostle were celebrating it. It was bathed in a deep supernaturality, similar, I imagined, to those old family-room Masses celebrated in the shadowed light of a turf fire in the wilds of western Ireland. So enchanting was the experience that Krista's eyes began to well with tears at the start of the Eucharistic Liturgy. When Monsignor Esseff slowly raised the Host with his fingers, hands, and arms worn down by arthritis and toil, tears ran down her cheek.

Noticing that Krista had been touched by the intimacy of the Mass, Monsignor Esseff began to speak softly with her off to the side afterward. She asked if he would anoint her. Inflamed with the love of a great-grandfather, he smiled and requested that they move into the sacristy.

In the silence of the small room, he pulled up a chair, placed it in front of Krista, and asked her to sit down. Thereafter, he stared deeply into her eyes for what seemed half a minute. Krista didn't know then that he was looking directly into the far-flung places of her soul.

After a long silence, he spoke: "Krista, why are you running?" She was stunned. "You've spent so much of your life running away from Jesus. And He has spent all of His time coming for you. He knocks on your door—and you slam the door in his face." The image of Father Flum on that winter night came immediately to mind, and tears welled.

"Jesus is asking you to stop and turn around and come to Him," he said in his gravelly voice. "You're running a marathon in the wrong direction." He grabbed hold of Krista's hands as tears ran down her cheeks. After a period of silence, he closed his eyes and began to speak in a voice entirely different in tone and rhythm, a pleading voice that no longer sounded the same. "Krista, please ... turn back to me. I have been waiting to love you your entire life. Come to me." He was speaking as Jesus Christ, *in persona Christi*, as if the Son of God had crawled into the skin of the ninety-two-year-old exorcist. Thereafter, Monsignor Esseff set his face like flint and stepped into the depths of Krista's soul, as if he had picked up a walking stick, and began to press into every corner. He began to pull memories from her as simply as he would have blessed a lunchtime meal, revealing long-held wounds.

He exposed the unconfessed drinking and began to needle into boils of trapped secrets and sin. As seeming pus released, Krista's tears fell.

Because he instinctively knew Krista was in the midst of experiencing an emotional whirlwind, he stopped speaking. He began to smile tenderly and love her through the warmth of his eyes. Thereafter he anointed and prayed over her. Silence permeated the small, sacred room. Before she left, the uncommon priest reminded Krista that she, too, was Jesus, and that it was time she began to walk back to Him, to be safe by His side.

Krista left the sacristy with reddened, dazed eyes, appearing like a ghost-haunted Ebeneezer Scrooge. As we were saying our goodbyes, Monsignor Esseff pulled Krista off to the side and spoke softly into her ear. "Your trip to Scranton wasn't for your husband's book. It was for you."

As I drove through rolling hills and mountains back to Maryland, we didn't speak about what had unfolded in the sacristy. Asking her about it would have been ridiculous. After some time, Krista spoke. "Before he anointed me, he looked into me—and it was Jesus who was speaking. It didn't *feel* like Jesus. It *was* Jesus who spoke and stood in front of me." She told me he addressed the parts of her she had either forgotten or never considered. An exorcist had read her soul as easily as if he had adjusted the cuff of his shirt.

In the days after returning home, we discovered the holy priest was renowned for reading souls. At a point in his conversation with Padre Pio fifty-nine years earlier, Monsignor Esseff confessed to the saint that he felt he was failing to draw out penitents' unrevealed mortal sins during the Sacrament of Reconciliation. Padre Pio gave a knowing smile to the young priest. He instructed then-Father

Esseff to begin to call on Padre Pio's own Guardian Angel when he struggled in the confessional, and he would metaphysically discharge him to Pennsylvania from his home in San Giovanni Rotondo in the northern part of Italy's heel. Thereafter, the young priest's confrontation with penitents' unconfessed grave sin ended.

Krista began to have long stretches of efflorescent days and weeks, when her soul seemed free from all turmoil. We attended weekday Masses together, and she read spiritual books by my side at night. At Father Flum's prompting, we prayed a month-long novena to Saint Joseph, where we agreed to abstain for thirty days from marital relations and alcohol. Krista told me how peaceful it felt to be united to me through prayer. Krista cried one night when she and I listened to the words of the Waterboys' "This Is the Sea."

> *Now I can see you wavering*
> *As you try to decide*
> *You've got a war in your head*
> *And it's tearing you up inside*
> *You're trying to make sense*
> *Of something that you just can't see*
> *Trying to make sense now*
> *And you know you once held the key*
> *But that was the river*
> *And this is the sea.*

Krista had come to hate indulging the swallowing rush of her impulses. She wanted the safe and pure places again, like the inviolable memories of her body melding with a hunter-jumper in midflight, the handhold of her Italian grandmother, and the noises and smells of her family's Italian restaurants, where her heart was lifted by the high-spirited banter, swirling aromas of tangy sauces, and comfort of her family's favorite booth. The kids saw joy in Mom's eyes. It was clear to all of us: Monsignor Esseff's work to purify and enlarge her soul spiritually had set her on a different path. Krista began to walk back, clear-eyed and sober.

Although the sharp edge of the Scranton mystic's spiritual weapon cut deep into the substratum of Krista's wounds, he had no spiritual tool for her will. In the sacristy, Monsignor Esseff had set in motion a sincere longing in her to be free, but the long walk back to the Father was one she would need to make on her own. Shame was too powerful. On a random night, Krista drank in secret. I returned home from a place long-forgotten and smelled wine in the room as Krista slept.

It was that summer that the loneliest months of our marriage blew in. In a supernatural realm, I felt Satan grip harder then; I felt viscerally his desire for the pure destruction of Krista and my family. Hyper-tuned to a daughter of God edging closer to freedom, he seemed to dispatch choruses of his most tormenting demons, who sang unmelodious sheet music into her soul—*You deserve it; no one gets you.*

Chapter 9

Velocity

Although Monsignor Esseff urged me to write, I couldn't. One side of my brain held my zeal; the other, an unsightly collection of rejection letters and emails politely suggesting my proposal was little more than an individual campaign to cast judgment on priests. After returning from Scranton, I'd rise each morning at 4:30 to write, but found that my fingers became like the small whirling blades of helicopters hovering over a small area of space above my keyboard. Nine years after a deceased priest and his earthbound friend worked to heal me, I had considered writing to priests to tell them *who they were* and unveil through stories the sacred methods of the holiest priests down the ages. The heart of the issue with publishers was that an old sports writer and masonry contractor was proposing curative solutions to a priest's spiritual amnesia.

And into the winter quarters of my office blew the internal commotion of the writer's blackest demon—everything became blocked. So each day until noon, for seven or so hours, I hovered over a screen with few words, as a helicopter does over a calamitous scene. Some days, I'd write down a string of paragraphs, where often I'd awaken the next morning, greeted by what seemed yesterday's muddied rivulets of sentences, and delete every word.

Meanwhile, Krista kept drinking most nights. In one room was a husband with writing feet of clay, in the other, a wife caught in her vice. Although Krista wasn't walking, I was every day. A new path was carved into the woods in front of my house; contractors poured asphalt along the grooved and overgrown path of an old railroad line. Around noon each day, before the kids returned from school, I made my way to the path, still mostly unknown except by those in the neighborhood. Krista rarely accompanied me, likely wary of what might be opened up in conversation along the way.

I always carried a Rosary but found my prayers often being interrupted by worrying thoughts of Krista's drinking, proper guardianship of my growing children, and my decision to leave work to write a book that my cluttered mind didn't seem to allow me the space to write. I remember I stopped praying the decades of the Rosary and began merely to thumb the beads, repeating over and over a plaintive refrain: *Mary, Mother me now. . . . Mary, Mother me now. . . . Mary, Mother me now.*

Near the end of the wooded path, I always stopped by an open field with a small two-horse barn. The old train track and path at this point were elevated, so passersby could look down into a sweeping panorama of the pasture and of the old farmhouse and large shade trees that framed the idyllic scene. Each time I arrived at this point, I leaned against a wooden fence and thought of my mom. The large farmhouse with dormer windows took me to her childhood home in an Italian section of Devon, a sleepy town on the Main Line, twenty miles outside of Philadelphia. As children, my brother and I would walk into the fields behind the home and take a dirt path leading to the railroad tracks where the "Paoli local" zipped by at high speeds. We'd lay out a few pennies on the rails and wait on the next train.

Alone on the path in the midst of what often seemed to me an existential spiral, I stared into the farmhouse and pasture that served as Elysian fields of memory, a pastoral image of warm and untroubled days. My gaze always fell upon a single white wrought-iron bench set below a large arm of a shade tree. The image of the empty bench sprang into my soul as a seeming signal grace, as it impregnated me with memories of Mom, who had died too early from cancer in 2013. Forty-five years earlier, Judy Wells sat on the same style of bench to watch me pump my legs on the large swing set in the backyard of her youth. At my highest point in the air, I would peek at Mom to make sure she knew her son was the bravest boy on earth. She would often give me a startled look—or so I thought then—pantomiming that the tips of my sneakers were getting too close to the surface of the sun.

As I leaned against the fence and looked into the re-membered image of Mom reclined beneath the shade tree, I saw her craning her head to look up at me. She saw her exhausted boy, and concern and empathy bathed her face. As I allowed the consolation of Mom's love to take hold, her pitying look turned into one of maternal instruction: *Patience, Kevin. God is very close to you now. Trust what I am saying. Love Krista in her trial. As she clung to you as you were dying, do the same for her in her unreachable place. As she believed you would live, trust she will, too.*

I was drawn to Krista because of her tender similarities to my mom. She was quiet and kept things simple. Neither put on pretenses or had any interest in the latest news, gossip, or fashion. Krista was perfectly content to while away her days quietly on the back of a horse stabled in the meadow behind her small one-bedroom countryside home. Mom would have seen a radiance woven into Krista's simplicity; her son's quiet future wife who stayed far away from a world of swirling motion and sense phenomena. But Mom, who was a humble prophet—her eight children have noted over the years—would have worried about Krista. She would have seen behind Krista's eyes, even then, unresolved wounds.

As I stood there looking at a ghost on an empty bench, I begged, often teary-eyed, for Mom's intercession. Were Mom still alive, I felt certain she would have taken Krista under her wing and striven to nurture her with the lone medicine that would disperse her pain; Mom would have softly hand-led Krista to the awareness of God's eternal love for her. But she was gone. When the last of her eight children, John, left the house, cancer took hold. One morning, far into the thickets of a cancer-ravaged body, she knelt at weekday Mass and couldn't get up. She turned to a fellow daily communicant and long-time friend seated behind her and allowed her sad eyes to explain the predicament. The woman lifted her from the kneeler. After that, death came swiftly.

I felt strongly then that Mom was mightily interceding for me. In a dimension stretching past the bounds of earth and intellect, I could actually *feel* Mom listening to each of my disconsolate words to her. In prayer then, she had sparked to life in me more often than my patron saints, Guardian Angel, and even Uncle Tommy. I saw Mom pleading at the feet of God, asking Him to help her little, lost boy keep pumping his legs.

I often visited a small Adoration chapel down the road from my house. Because I had grown tired of considering my plight, and asking God for resolve, I found myself falling into a new routine. Rather than reclining at one of the twenty or so chairs and kneelers, I knelt at the foot of the small altar, stretched my arm out, and placed my fingertips on the base of the monstrance. Following the way of the mind-emptying Tibetan monk, I closed my eyes and strove to cast away every thought. When the images

came—Krista's indomitable vice and my children's awareness, my dead-end book and sudden joblessness—I worked
to push them out instantly and onto the foot of the monstrance. I thought one day in prayer: I am the hemorrhaging woman two thousand years later.

Although Krista's drinking and shame clung to her like
deer ticks, operations of grace did move within me, or at
least worked to reorient me with the Cross. Perhaps it was
exhaustion from the pattern of life, but I felt my own cross
of loneliness begin to rejuvenate and urge me to bind it
with Christ's own Cross, where at least if progress wasn't
made, I could still hide myself in His wounds.

Within the intimacy, I felt my interior misery and endless strategizing slowly peel away, as I spoke as a small
child would to his daddy from the Cross. I clung to Jesus
there and asked that He permeate and free me to love Him
from the Cross. I wanted to love Krista from the Cross as
He did, to pour myself out entirely for her, as He did—
without complaint, with only surrendering love.

Father Flum kept meeting with Krista. She would bring
him fresh eggs from our chickens, cartons of whole milk,
and occasional dinners and soups as a way of thanking him
for his persistence. She sometimes cleaned the entire rectory. Father Flum called me every so often to suggest that
I was taking part, in a sense, in the same crucifixion of
the scandal-marred Church. He encouraged me to refrain
from overeagerness in speeding along Krista's healing and
to press on with a calm spirit. He told me Krista was making great progress in ways that were difficult to gauge and
that I would struggle to see. If I held firm in patiently
loving Krista and stood my ground with hopeful surrender
to God's mysterious plan, he said, the winter thaw would
come. He promised it was coming.

Month followed month. I pecked away at the keys on
my laptop and did what I could as a husband and father

to keep the wolf from the door of my soul and family. To counteract the temptation to project into what I might have regarded as a bleak future, I awakened each day as recovering alcoholics are encouraged to do. I focused on the task at hand for that day alone. And there were small indicators and signposts of hope. I was beginning to see deep pain in Krista when she fell; angst was written on her face that revealed a hatred for what she was doing to herself and our family. From my office window, I would occasionally see her facing away from me and into our open field, where she sat on a small chair in front of the statue of Our Lady. The image was a cairn of God's subtle movement. Now and then she would join me on an evening walk on the path, where we would stop at the farmhouse, while I shared some childhood memories. I pointed to the two-horse barn and spoke to her about how it reminded me of when we first met.

One summer evening, with the kids scattered about at friends' homes and the community pool, I asked Krista if she wanted to watch a movie. She agreed. I told her I'd pick up some subs and asked that she pick out a movie while I was gone. When, thirty minutes later, I stepped through the door, she was on the couch, avoiding eye contact. She had been drinking, I knew.

"Did you find a movie?" I asked, placing the subs on the table in front of her.

"Why do you always ask me to find one?" she said, disturbed. "You find a movie. You're the one who wanted to watch one."

"Krista, come on," I asked, stepping back into the trap of attempted rational conversation. "What's going on here?"

A fight ensued, which we had worked hard to avoid since I had begun to stay home. Memory doesn't permit me to recall the exchange of words, but something happened that hadn't before. After fifteen or so minutes of

back-and-forth, Krista left the family room and retreated
to our bedroom. I went into the backyard, where the colors of the summer sky were fading into twilight. After
some time, I went back inside where I saw Krista sitting in
front of a laptop in the dining room.

"If you really think I'm this bad, and I need to go
away," she said, angrily, "then I will." She showed me
the page she was opened to; it was a rehabilitation center.
I was flabbergasted. I quickly worked to compose myself
and internally praised God.

"Well," I said. "Can I help?" No answer. I slowly pulled
a chair close to her.

For the next hour, we searched out places, Krista in
trepidation, and I in silent awe. We barely spoke a word as
we researched for perhaps the most consequential hour in
our eighteen years of marriage. I remember begging God
that Krista wouldn't suddenly turn on her idea and get up
and leave. I also begged God to keep me from saying anything that would disturb what we were pursuing.

We found what seemed a solid place in the midwestern
states. "What do you think?" I asked. "They seem like
the ones with the best approach. It seems like they com-
bine treatment with faith. And it looks like Mass is offered
every day."

"If you think so," she said. "Do whatever you want."
She got up from the table and went to bed.

I emailed the center, asking for admittance the following day.

I awakened early the next morning holding my breath.
"Krista, they are expecting us later this evening," I said.
"We should talk about how to share this with the kids."

After some attempts to backpedal and promises to work
to stop drinking, Krista saw that I wasn't budging from
what she had committed to. She began to sob, in a fashion

I had never seen. Some things you never forget. I held her as she wept. After a long while, she looked at me and spoke, "I'll pack and then we'll tell them." Her watery, reddened eyes shone with a mother's humiliated heart split in two, the broken eyes of one set to go off and die.

After bringing her suitcase into the foyer, I told her I would awaken the kids. From a window in Shannon's bedroom, I could see Krista pacing back and forth in the morning shadows beneath the enormous elm in our front yard. I couldn't see that she was on her cell phone. In her torment, she had called Father Flum to tell him what she was about to do. Much later, she shared his words that day: "I know you're scared. But you have the strength for this—and your kids need to see it in you now. Krista, Our Lady will be with you when you tell them."

After I had gathered the kids in the family room, I saw Krista in the backyard near the statue of Our Lady of Lourdes. I remember she had on a powder-blue Mustard Seed t-shirt and faded red shorts with a white stripe down the sides. She had set up two empty chairs about six feet across from her, one for me, the other for a child. Krista wanted to speak with each one individually, beginning with Gabby, the oldest. I remember walking out with her on the sunny morning. Birdsong filled the air and a lawn-mower buzzed in the distance. A few minutes later, Gabby listened to her mom tell her she would be leaving in a few hours to enter a rehabilitation center. Tears immediately sprang into Gabby's eyes. In a startling fashion that seemed to me then purely of God, Krista maintained a certain peace. She told Gabby in measured words that she was sick and needed to get well for her and the rest of us.

"Gabby, I am sorry for not being a good mom," she said. Tears blurred my eyes. "I'll do my best to come back as the mom you deserve." Krista's resolve finally gave way, and tears came. Knowing she couldn't allow herself to fall apart, Krista stiffened and looked at Gabby with earnestness. In those few seconds, it seemed to me, she had managed muscularly to will her humiliation and shame away in order to command Gabby. She told her eldest daughter she needed to become a mother-like presence for Sean and Shannon. She said I was going to need her help while she was away. Through her heaving tears, Gabby assured her she would do her best. As they clutched onto each other, I looked back into the house and saw Sean and Shannon, who looked on in confusion through the bay window.

Next came stoic Sean, who said the most wonderful thing. After Krista apologized for having to leave home to seek help, Sean said, "Mom, your leaving to get better shows me that you're not sick, but that you're well. No one who was sick would think to do something like what you're doing for us." Sean's words startled me, as if he had spent the entire night scripting them. They became instant poems, written indelibly into his mom's broken soul. He could have said nothing more befitting. Krista asked Sean to promise to be strong for her and to pay close attention to Shannon, his sister who looked up to him.

Oh, man. Shannon. I should have asked Gabby to return to the family room to be with Shannon while Krista spoke with Sean, but I had forgotten. I saw her looking into the disconsolate scene from the window, like a child who'd strayed and lost sight of her family in Grand Central Station. She was standing beside Zeus, the 200-pound Saint Bernard, twice her size, who slept by her side on her narrow bed each night. Seeing them asleep together was a nightly comedy sketch; he often had an enormous front leg wrapped around her face.

When I came to get her, I was looking into the wide eyes of a frightened doe. She was standing by the couch, where we had spent countless dozens of early evenings sitting beside one another watching *Little House on the Prairie* episodes. Earlier that year, she had written a letter in pencil in her best handwriting to Melissa Gilbert, the actress who played "Half-pint." She told the actress she was her favorite character, uncomprehending that Gilbert was now a fifty-something woman nearly forty years removed from the show. The hours upon hours of midwestern order seemed then a diabolic inverse of the valley of sadness I was hand-leading her to in the backyard.

Krista kept her poise and spoke with feathered grace, as if her angel had guided her words and held her together. Shannon did her best to understand the parts of what her eleven-year-old mind wouldn't permit her to process. With Gabby and Sean beside their mom like newly recruited soldiers of support, Krista told Shannon she had been battling a sickness and that the summer months provided the perfect time for the healing she needed. She assured her that her sickness would be gone in no time. Shannon listened intently, and wept small tears, wearing the look of Half-pint, whose Ma carefully broke to her the news of the death of her favorite calf. A few hours later, I took a single photograph of the day that is still buried in the cloud recesses of my cell phone. It is of Shannon with her arms wrapped fully around her mom's waist outside of a busy airport.

Four hours later, we followed the GPS in our rental car past miles of cornfields that led to a sprawling ranch-style home hemmed in by grassy fields and wide-open acres of seemingly endless farmland. We stepped out of the car to the summer hum of insects that broke the silence of the tension. I grabbed Krista's suitcase in one hand and her own hand with my other. I don't know if I had ever loved her more than at that moment, as we walked up the sidewalk that led to the front entrance.

Reality set in instantly; Krista was asked for her cell phone, and I was politely asked to leave for ninety or so minutes while Krista underwent an intake evaluation. I found a winsome screened-in gazebo out front, but the smell of cigarettes immediately sent me out. I saw a picnic table on a grassy field in the distance. I walked to it beneath white clouds streaking a swallowing blue sky. I sat down and called Gabby, telling her that her mom was doing great and that I'd be home later that night. She told me that all was fine at home; Shannon was at the pool with friends and Sean was working a shift at Chick-fil-A. She told me she had kept close to Shannon after we left.

"She is quiet about it," Gabby said. "And I didn't press her. I just made her feel like Mom would be home soon and completely well."

"Great job, Gab," I said. "She will be."

After we disconnected, I called Father Flum and told him Krista was in the process of being admitted to a rehabilitation center. I told him religious Sisters daily visited the center and that I had already seen one enter the place. He told me Krista had called with the news earlier that day and that he had been in prayer about it all. He wanted to know the name of the center and asked me particular questions about its methods of treatment. He asked about the state of Krista's and my mind, then asked about the kids.

"Krista seems to be okay, like she wants it," I said. "I'm okay. It's the kids, of course, who are on my mind."

"How about I come out to the house tomorrow?" he suggested. "I'll bring the chainsaws, and we'll work on cutting up the tree that fell in your backyard." A huge tree had fallen a few days earlier in the back field. "That would be great, Father Flum." We hung up, and I pulled my Rosary out of my pocket and prayed looking into a cornfield.

Krista found me a while later and led me to her room, where she introduced me to her roommate, a pleasant woman from Florida. She told me she would be allowed to attend daily Mass; she seemed in better spirits than I had anticipated. Before I knew it, it was time for me to leave and for Krista to attend her first session.

In the small parking lot, I told her I had never been as proud of her and that she was a hero to her kids and me. She was wearing blue jeans and a gray and white striped sweater as we hugged for a long while. She smiled through tears, looked at me through red-rimmed eyes, and told me I had a plane to catch.

As I backed the car out of the lot, I saw her standing alone and still with a bereaved look. A vast cornfield framed the scene behind her. She held a leather-bound Magnificat in her right hand; her left was lifted in the air to wave goodbye. From my rearview mirror, she resembled a small scarecrow falling apart and on the wrong side of the fence; her waving arm seemed made of straw. Feelings of unbearably tender love poured into me for her, my suffering wife whom I wouldn't see again for six weeks.

Chapter 10

Pressing Down

After celebrating morning Mass at his parish, Father Flum drove up in his pick-up the next morning. It was one of the many times he had been to our home since Krista slammed the door on him. He walked to the front door with a pair of oil-smeared chainsaws. I had never before seen him outside of his cassock; his body was seemingly enfleshed by a pair of tan, long-sleeve, full-body coveralls. With his beard spilling over the top layer of the Dickies protective wear, he resembled an Amish farmer.

"Let's get to that tree," he said.

For the next several hours, on a typically high-eighties, humid Maryland summer morning, Father Flum and I went to work. With muscles rippling through his taut forearms, he directed the heavy chainsaw as effortlessly as thurible swings. The growling buzz of the saw prevented either of us from speaking. Our lone communication was hand gestures or a movement of the eyes when he wanted a fresh-cut block of wood pulled away for another cut. Sweat poured down our faces and bodies.

With the job completed in the early afternoon, I went inside to get large mason jars of cold iced tea. He declined an offer for lunch. When I walked back outside with the tea, he was seated at the grotto on one of the two small chairs in front of the statue of Mary. I sat in the chair beside him and handed him the mason jar. He took large swallows through his tremendous beard and placed the jar on the ground. Neither of us spoke. He looked into the visage of Mary, to whom he had consecrated his priesthood.

After a long period of silence, he spoke into the space in front of him. He said Krista's admittance was the time for me to increase my prayer and fasting. He told me to stay intensely close to the kids and to strive each day to maintain my joy and calm while in their presence.

"Speak openly to them when they ask you questions," he said, turning to face me. "Give straightforward answers. Say exactly what their heart is telling them to do, and that is to pray for their mom. Tell them that their prayers are necessary now."

Thereafter, he allowed the music of silence, knowing I needed to contemplate his words. The trills of birds, the buzzing of summertime insects, and far-off dog barks were the only noise for an extended period of time. Sweat continued to run down our faces.

Thereafter, he closed his eyes and led us in a long prayer, in which he asked Our Lady to promote Krista's full recovery. He lightly slapped his thighs and stood up to leave. As I walked him to his truck, he asked if I wouldn't mind sharing with him the phone number of the rehabilitation center.

In the days that followed, strange things began to happen.

On a volcano-hot afternoon, I drove Shannon to a toy store to buy crafts. She had spent some of her time since Krista's absence piecing together small wooden boats, airplanes, and the like. After pulling in to park, a car suddenly tore into the space next to us—just as Shannon was opening the passenger-side door. The driver slammed into the door, barely missing Shannon's right leg. After my own car jerked forward, I jumped back in to check on Shannon, who fell back into her seat. When I looked frantically to see if she had been hit, the driver gunned her car in reverse and raced from the parking lot, wheels squealing on the hot asphalt. The entire event took place in a span of seconds.

"Were you hit? Are you all right?" I asked, completely unnerved.

"She didn't hit me," Shannon said, saucer-eyed. "Why did she leave?" She said she looked into a woman's eyes. "She was young."

Two days later, Zeus, our enormous Saint Bernard puppy at just over two years of age, began to limp around the house. I thought he might have stepped into a back-yard hole. The limp worsened. After dinner one night, I loaded him into the back of our minivan, where Shannon kept her gargantuan bedmate company.

We spent the next three hours at a veterinary hospi-tal. A few hours into the visit, a tender-eyed veterinarian called me—not Shannon—back into an X-ray room. As I stepped into the small room, Zeus was on a large table, his fat tail wagging. The technician pointed to the gray mass that covered the screen, the one that was thinning Zeus' front left leg. He had advanced cancer that was spreading into the rest of his body. "His leg may snap," she warned. "The leg could be removed, but he would be carrying a lot of weight. It might be a hard way to go for Zeus." She advised putting him to sleep might be the most humane option. "This leg cancer is common for big dogs, even for young ones like Zeus."

Night had fallen when I walked back into a waiting room that had emptied. Shannon was sitting alone on a chair. "Is Zeus going to be okay?" she asked, still imagin-ing his limp was a result of an awkward step. "What did the doctor say?"

I lied. "They're still trying to figure things out." I told her the truth a few weeks later, the day before a mobile veterinarian came to our house with a satchel containing needles and a large vial of pentobarbital. While the kids were asleep that morning, I dug a large hole in the backyard, fifteen feet from the grotto, in between thorny rose bushes and a wild-armed yellow forsythia.

After the vet's sedative slowly rocked Zeus to sleep, we gathered around, knelt, and stroked his huge body, saying our goodbyes. A minute later, Zeus' heart stopped. As I dragged him into his place of rest, Shannon found a flat rock and wrote with an indelible marker, "To Zeus, the world's greatest dog." She wrote "R.I.P." and the dates of his birth and death, and when I was done shoveling in, she set the stone on top of the loose soil. She was inconsolable. I took her to Dairy Queen and told her to get the sloppiest and biggest ice cream they had, but she struggled to eat it.

Three or four days later, I looked outside and noticed five turkey vultures thumping their massive wings fifteen feet above the grave. And I became furious with myself for not digging the hole deeper. They circled for hours. Occasionally a vulture swooped down and stood on the upturned soil, standing directly on Shannon's small stone of farewell. The next day, I gathered sixty or so large field stones and piled them onto the soil above Zeus. The vultures didn't come back.

Despite attempts to keep things light in our home, it grew quiet. I couldn't domesticate or make merry the spreading blunt-force strangeness of Mom's absence. So even as I tried to keep upbeat, it seemed every step I took came on a tightrope that could snap at any time. I had quit sweeping the floors. When the kids weren't spending time with friends, Gabby and Sean had summer jobs behind cash registers to keep them occupied. Shannon and I were well into *Little House* reruns. She didn't ask many questions about her mom, trusting in the sacrosanct world of a child who knows her mom is getting better and would soon be home, without caring about the circumstances behind her being gone.

Krista and I wrote to each other through the mail, as we did when we were boyfriend and girlfriend. When she came home later that summer, she came holding a Saint Bernard puppy we named Eddie after a baseball player who was my childhood hero. On her drive home in a car she had rented, she had made the purchase of the puppy. The kids engulfed their mom with hugs and began to work on loving a new dog. Life resumed, and we held out unspoken hope that her time away helped to cast out the disorder to allow space for the recreation of her soul.

It was around then that a publisher picked up my manuscript on priestly renewal. I had written it just before the shadow of the American Catholic Church's summer of shame in 2018, when the McCarrick scandal, Pennsylvania grand jury report, and other evils committed by those within the Church poured onto the Catholic landscape like Old Testament plagues. The timing was providential.

But the joy of a book deal quickly became overshadowed by the growing tension in our home. Within a few weeks of her return home, Krista grew quieter—and the familiar feeling of our hardwood floors beginning to feel like unsteady planks returned; a collapse, I preternaturally knew, would be coming soon. The reemergence of what seemed an unconquerable demon in the tall weeds of our home began to follow Krista—and all of us in some fashion—from room to room. Gabby and Sean felt it and, on separate occasions, clumsily brought their mom's anxiousness to my attention. I attempted to encourage them that Mom was adjusting to a new beginning and that things would sort themselves out, though, as much as I hated to admit it to myself, I knew the opposite was true.

One morning, on the back patio, I asked Krista if anything was bothering her or if there was anything painful she needed to release. After a period of silence, she told me she resented that I had "sent her away." I replied, perhaps too quickly, "Krista, we decided this together. And you sat in those chairs and told the kids you were doing it for them. They see you as a hero for them." She immediately rejected the notion, but I swore to its accuracy. Her eyes narrowed. And the old fight came back, with invisible demons hovering—I imagined—and hanging on each syllable.

Man, I thought, *it's back.*

After sitting quietly a while, she looked into the backyard, seemingly recollecting her memories of that day. She admitted to me that her shame "at being sent away" was eating her alive. She said she felt humiliated. We spoke about her treatment, and she shared that clinicians spent little time attempting to address the long-held wounds of her shame and feelings of never measuring up. She assured me that she didn't feel a desire to drink secretly. "I can't get out of my own head," she said, downcast. "I know I need to give my humiliation to God and move on. But the shame is stuck in me now."

A thought came to me with piercing clarity. I extemporaneously floated it into the heavy air. "What about we call Monsignor Esseff? He'd want to hear everything you've just been through," I suggested, knowing of the indelible mark he had made in her. "Would you want to share your thoughts with him? I'll call him up."

"You can try," she said before leaving to go inside. "I'd like to see him."

I reached for my cell and called the exorcist. He answered on the third ring. The door to the pit beneath my feet closed up.

"Hello, Monsignor Esseff," I said. "Kevin Wells here." I was blessed; he remembered Krista and me. At the time of the phone call, he had committed his life to the spiritual direction of priests, who flew from throughout the country into Pennsylvania to seek his spiritual guidance and wisdom on three-day directed retreats. For the first time in six decades, he was no longer directing laity.

"I have a favor to ask of you," I said tentatively. "I'd like for you to meet with Krista. She's in trouble."

After a period of silence, he responded through the haze in his husky voice, asking a single question that sounded like a miracle. "Can she make it up today?"

"Yes," I said. "We'll get her on the road within the hour. Expect her at around 2:30."

I disconnected and went inside. "Krista, Monsignor Esseff would like to see you," I said. "He wants to know if you can make it up his way right now." She paused and then retreated to our bedroom.

Ten minutes later, she said goodbye and walked out the front door to make the four-hour drive to Scranton. As the car pulled from our driveway, tears sprung in my eyes. I didn't know any more if tears came because of the bits of the manna God brought in the storm or because of the constancy of the marital strain. No matter, as she steered our car west toward the Pennsylvania mountains, I knew the heel of Satan had at least temporarily lifted from Krista's and my throats. I couldn't have imagined a better place for Krista to be than with a holy man who knew the tactics of Satan in attacking a humiliated soul as well as anyone on earth.

The priest warmly welcomed Krista into his small living space, a room partially taken up by his floor-to-ceiling-length pale brown coffin leaning up against a corner in his room, a daily reminder of his death. He placed a chair in front of him and asked Krista to sit. The former boxer who had fought demons throughout numberless exorcisms down the years sat quietly and looked into Krista's eyes. Right away, she told him that she had recently spent time at a rehabilitation clinic. Krista told me a few years later that she spoke of her angst and shared with the priest that I was overly critical. She told him that she was struggling to attain peace amidst her mountain of shame. After some time, Monsignor Esseff closed his eyes and asked if she wanted to confess her sins, to which Krista agreed.

After confessing her final sin, he allowed a period of silence to permeate the space between them. After a disquieting period of noiselessness, he opened his eyes and, with deep resonance in his tone, slowly asked a single question. "Would you like to know the sins you didn't confess?"

Startled, Krista paused, then nodded, hesitantly. His look was a combination of sobriety and love as he told my wife something she had never heard. "You are arrogant," he said. "And it is a pus. You've wanted life on your terms, without concern for God's wants. It is a self-pitying pus that you've carried." An ax had been flung into her heart as a wave of weariness seeped into all parts of her. She sat wide-eyed as the priest brought to the surface what seemed to her to be miles and miles of unconfessed and unconsidered sin.

But as he spoke, the broadside of the exposition of her buried sins, curiously, felt lovingly delivered. Although the mystic priest's words carried an exactness, it wasn't a woodshed whipping she felt as he dusted off the list of her unobserved sin. His manner and tone seemed administered within the hearth-fire warmth of a humble country inn, where a silver tray of steaming tea, country meats and cheeses, and fresh bread was set aside, awaiting her by a peat fire. Throughout the confession, his soft, husky voice seemed like the lifting of wood smoke, a soothing incantation designed to raise long-forgotten and unknown trespasses. His eyes were soft and carried a deeper measure of love. Monsignor Esseff seemed then to Krista to be a shepherd among pastures of lilies; she was the broken lamb sprawled upon his shoulders.

After absolving my wife's sins, he rested his palms on his lap, closed his eyes, and remained quiet to allow Krista time to gather herself. After some time, he began to stroke his bushy gray goatee and speak to her in a voice carved out of nearly a century of prayer. He directed her to scriptural passages and spiritual tools and mechanisms that would help her subdue all that had been revealed. "Krista, I want you to know something that is very important. God the Father has loved you from the beginning of time, since before creation, since before He created Adam and Eve," he told her in a voice barely more than a whisper as he echoed Father Flum's words to her. "When you begin to open up to the depths of God's love, you'll begin to know what it is to become His daughter. You will know His peace. And you will know His love and will for you."

It was time to leave and drive back to Maryland. Krista stood on wobbly legs and watched as Monsignor Esseff slowly pushed off from his chair and stepped slowly toward her. He flung out his arthritic arms and smiled the radiant smile of saints. They embraced for a long while in silence, like Christ holding on tightly to His Mother after step-ping away from the tomb. Krista pushed out a thank-you through tears. But the priest wasn't done with his work. The scalpel into her woundedness required additional spiritual expository work. "What time will you be back tomorrow?" he asked. She hadn't anticipated a second meeting; she hadn't packed an overnight bag.

"Will the same time work tomorrow?" Krista asked.

"I'll be waiting for you," he said. "Today was tough. But it was wonderful as well." He looked at Krista warmly, as if she were his first love.

She checked into a room at the Dunmore Inn like a soldier shot in a war. She spent the remainder of the evening in a rupture of tears, where raw self-awareness flowed through her like a river. He had called her "arrogant," which she had never once considered.

The following day Monsignor Esseff asked if she could manage to pull away from her family for the remainder of the week, where together they could work to uncover underlying wounds and work to overcome them. Krista called me and asked if it would be okay to stay for four additional days with Monsignor Esseff. I said "yes" faster than cannon fire. When she returned home, her face shone an amalgam of baptismal innocence and trepidation, like the shy first-grader making her uneasy appearance on the first day of school.

"Kevin, I'm ready to try again," Krista told me. "I was told things about myself I needed to be told." Her eyes cast resoluteness, and showed what seemed a true desire for an external shift to health. In a sense, she had been scared straight, ferried by a priest through dark seas and into a safe place for docking.

She drove out to Father Flum's country parish and poured out in a flood tide what Monsignor Esseff had revealed in her to her. The bearded priest smiled knowingly and suggested they begin to meet more frequently for spiritual direction. In the meantime, he encouraged Krista to commit to weekly confessions, pray daily Rosaries, attend weekday Masses, and spend time with nightly spiritual reading. She obliged each, and soon peace began to settle in her as if sheets of poetry dropped from Heaven and into her soul. He began to call her more often from his flip phone to check on her as he traveled in his pick-up from one place to another.

Unexpectedly, toward the end of 2019, Krista began to awaken regularly at 3 A.M.—most nights to the exact minute. She felt stalked and overcome by heaviness and darkness. After a few weeks of experiencing the phenomenon, she told Monsignor Esseff, who encouraged her to begin immediately praying the Rosary. He told her the 3 A.M. hour was a threatening, but efficacious, hour. "Keep a Rosary under your pillow, and pray to Mary as soon as you awaken; it is the hour her Son releases souls from Purgatory. And it is the devil's hour." I would occasionally awaken in darkness to the soft sound of a Rosary being prayed.

One day, I discovered Krista had drunk the night before. When I told her I knew, I saw in her eyes, for the first time, the look of a scared child, as if she were being pulled downstream into a place no one could get to. Surprisingly, she didn't respond angrily. Rather than her eyes being dimmed by shame, they pleaded for my help. She clearly hated what she had done. Thereafter, she told me—as best as she was able—the inner movements that had led to the backslide. I do not recall the specifics of what she shared, but as she unpacked it, I remember thinking, for the first time, that I knew she wanted to be completely free. I held her and said little. "You are beating this," I said. "And the devil is going to come hard now. But we will beat this."

A few weeks later, two priests prayed over Krista in a session of Unbound, a prayer ministry designed to renounce and take authority over evil spirits.

Although there were periodic falls, Krista made it a habit to drive out to Father Flum's parish the following day to confess the fall. Most days, before arriving at his parish, she pulled into the small lot of the local post office to park her car, bang the steering wheel, and cry tears of shame. After some time of steeling herself, she drove off to step into Father Flum's small confessional and unburden her sin. When she shared with me her post-office stops, and her resilience to see the confession through, I knew an inner transformation was quietly beginning to unfold in her. She told me, as best as she was able, the manner that graces were beginning to sanctify the fears, shame, and dark corners in her. She shared with me that she had become repulsed with drinking and her wounds. "I used to love the darkness and secrecy," she told me. "I wanted to live there. I cannot stand those places in me now."

Father Flum saw for the first time that Krista ached to break from her binge drinking. But he also knew that, despite her attendance at daily Mass and regularly confessing her sins, she needed greater help. They discussed the power of Satan, and that he would work hard to manipulate her. Where Monsignor Esseff and he continually pointed Krista to God's immense love for her, forces within her still had sway, pointing her back to her wounds. He asked her one day after confession if she would consider meeting with a Catholic counselor, a long-time friend of his. Krista agreed, and he suggested that I should also attend each session. We didn't know at the time that the counselor was an expert of uncovering and freeing people from deep layers of pain.

We fell immediately in love with the counselor's gentle way of scalpelling directly into wounds neither Krista nor I knew we had. After softening the ground of our hearts, he asked us to swivel our chairs and to face one another and explain our single deepest need. Sitting just a few feet across from me, Krista began. Through tears, she told me she needed me to believe in her and that she could be free one day from drinking. She told me that until she saw pure confidence in me, she would likely struggle. In response, I told her I had no doubt that she would be fully free and that I had never been prouder of her. She began to cry.

I shared my need: "Keep fighting to be a healthy and happy mom to our children." Through tears, she said, "I promise that I will, Kevin," We embraced one another for a long time. And in that single moment in time, it seemed to me that covens of long-circling demons vaporized in midair.

When I approached the desk for payment after the session, I was told that a donor would be paying the fee for each of our sessions.

Future sessions weren't always as rosy; not all the work of demons had gone away. With impatience, I expressed irritation over an occasional "bad night." I was then redirected to what I had promised Krista in our opening session; that I knew she could be well. It was clear to me that Krista was exhausted with her periodic falls and that she had chosen the right paths to attain full healing—counseling and the Church's goldmine provision of sacramental graces. She was attending daily Mass and confessing her sins two or three times a month, or whenever it was that she fell.

Perhaps because it seemed Krista was so close to freedom, the falls felt worse to me then, like the major league pitcher who spends the winter strengthening a surgically repaired shoulder and re-injuring it the first week of spring training.

We brought this dynamic into March of 2020, when COVID came like the swing of a hatchet.

Chapter 11

The Chariot That Carried Us Away

Like our first broken heart, each of us is likely to remember the day the pandemic lowered its horns to gore us. It drew first blood for me at a presentation I was asked to give by a religious order in Old Towne Alexandria, Virginia, on the manuscript I had written, *The Priests We Need to Save the Church*. The book was published on the Feast of the Assumption in 2019, and perhaps because my written plea for holy priests was released shortly after the red tide of clergy scandals, the book was selling well. Several priests from around the country and beyond began to contact me to say how the sacred characteristics and portrayals of priestly exceptionalism mentioned in the book had pierced and humbled them. Some said it had re-engineered their priesthood.

I was introduced to the reality of COVID-19 at exactly 7 P.M. on March 12, 2020, when I approached the lectern to begin the presentation. I recall looking into a sea of empty chairs that never filled. My memory is of eight people attending, half of them religious Sisters. After my talk, a softhearted Sister whispered to me, "They must have stayed home because of the virus."

The runaway locomotive burst through my mind, though; the memory that froze me on my drive home was the breaking story at the top of the 10 P.M. news hour.

Cardinal Wilton Gregory of the Archdiocese of Washington had announced earlier that afternoon the cancellation of Masses for the upcoming weekend. The reporter quoted the cardinal's words from the Archdiocese of Washington's press release: "My number one priority as your archbishop is to ensure the safety and health of all who attend our Masses."

The cardinal, it seemed to me—from his very first statement on the pandemic—had gotten it wrong. His "number one priority," I thought on that unforgettable drive, should be on the care of souls and not "the [worldly] safety and health of his flock." It seemed to me the mania of the virus had perhaps steered him from remembering his truest identity. Soon, it came to me, and I imagine many others that night, a sheet, like a blanket of volcanic ash, would fall on and cover over the sacraments worldwide.

From the dawn of the pandemic, the Church revealed her manner of approach: she would dictate and mandate the priority of the human body and the physical realm over the supernatural and the fate of the eternal soul. By Cardinal Gregory's quick-strike shutdown, he telegraphed what would become the Church's immediate response to the pandemic: she would show an unwillingness to find creative ways to continue to administer the sacraments and keep alive the celebration of Masses, while also allowing for the well-formed individual to consider the implications on physical health and safety. Submission to secular governmental dictates became far more important than the God-given authority to shepherd and lead the Church through the sacramentally ordained ministry of priest, prophet, and king.

On the drive home, a single question blew through me. *What of Krista—and all the Kristas?*

She and my family's thread of hope for her total recovery were the ancient medicines of the Church. The spiritual lifelines were saving her. She did all but spill her blood at weekly confessions when she coughed up and *owned* another fall. The graces of absolution were changing her; she felt it, and I saw it. She had started spending dedicated hours at Adoration, where she began to fall in love with both Our Lady and Jesus. She told me once her place to pray at Adoration was midway between the monstrance and a statue of Mary because she wanted to be "collapsed" by their love. And, most importantly, of course, Christ was carving small revolutions of hope, spiritual instruction, and embracing love into her soul at weekday and Sunday Masses.

Krista also came to realize the emotional highs she had experienced on mission trips and pilgrimages had failed. And, despite our counselor's noble and warmhearted efforts, Krista's periodic falls had made therapy sessions fractious. Her spiritual sustenance, what was truly bringing peace and a release of her desire to drink, was regular reception of the Eucharist and the Sacrament of Confession, where unseen graces managed to flow through her like rivers. Whether she would be receiving the Host or confessing to Father Flum, she was forced to probe deeply into her soul. It was those raw self-assessments, she told me, that helped provide her with a sacred ordering and feeling of peace.

Within a few days, though, it seemed the Kingdom of God was being conquered by a precocious brat, a baby demon who got whatever he pointed his little talon to. In the heart of the Church's most penitential season, the virus had managed to paralyze and shut down the worldwide Catholic Church, which had, stunningly, mostly bent her knee, diocese by diocese, across the world and nation, to the government-issued edicts to control people in the name of controlling a virus. The Church had amalgamated, seamlessly it seemed that Lenten season, with supernatural-less governments and schools, the media, and mostly unseen panels of doctors.

Whether folks considered the Church closures and cancellation of Masses prudent or incautious, in mere days, a Church-swung ax had been dropped into the souls of the millions of faithful Catholics who ordered their lives around the Mass and sacraments. Those Catholics who considered the weight of eternal realities and spiritual health over worldly peril—the set that viewed their own sin deadlier than even a killing virus—had been seemingly orphaned overnight. The fire of the sacramental graces that for years had kindled their souls had been blown out like racks of Tenebrae candles.

It can be imagined, at the dawn of the wide-sweeping worldwide panic, that those with the supernatural inner eye of J. R. R. Tolkien, Padre Pio, and author Michael O'Brien understood what the moratorium on the Church's indomitable sacraments would give birth to: the congealing of an unseen dark gathering. No one, though, knew then how rapidly and blatantly these unseen forces would manifest themselves in the culture at large. In short order, the rampaging and self-described atheistic Black Lives Matter and Antifa movements would pour into the nation's streets and conscience. Nationwide torchings of inner cities, the decapitations of Catholic statuary, the defacing of churches, the firebombing of crisis pregnancy centers, and vowed "nights of rage" would become the standard fare of the evening news. The demonization of the unvaccinated would in itself become a contagion that metastasized faster than California brushfires among most of the world's globalist secular lords, political leaders, mass media, doctors, and pop-culture celebrities. It seemed a strange symmetry when Pope Francis and many Catholic bishops and local parish priests eagerly hitched their wagon to those global forces, despite vaccines being mostly untested and some being traced to aborted fetal tissue. A fair number in the Church hierarchy, though, would soon become active in stigmatizing its unvaccinated faithful as selfish and unloving of their neighbor.

If history is correct, it is said that the overnight theft of a pig in West Virginia instigated the mountainside war in West Virginia between the Hatfield and McCoy families. In 2020, an ideological war seemed to ignite when united globalists aimed to steal the free will and well-formed consciences of humanity.

As it concerned the Church, I remember wondering then if most Catholics forgot or ceased to consider how a sustained sacramental famine might give wide berth for the Lawless One to send raw and menacing choruses of demons to accelerate an annihilation of reason, order, and the paradosis of two thousand years. I telephoned some grieving local priests and another exorcist, who each told me that COVID-19 and the absence of the sacraments had unleashed intense demonic activity. In an article, I quoted a priest known for his cheerfulness, work ethic, and devotion to Our Lady. "A great heaviness has entered into my priesthood. This time has been the biggest test of my priesthood, and I guess of my life," he said. "I do think the Evil One is hitting the priests hardest now. His number one tool is his spirit of discouragement. His M.O. is to make it seem like we're accomplishing nothing as a priest. Why pray? Why sit by the window [for outdoor confessions] when no one comes? Why make another [senseless] video on the need for prayer during COVID-19 when no one watches? It's like his voice says, 'You're worthless now as a priest—you're detached from your people, and they aren't praying or paying attention anyway.'" The exorcist told me this: "Satan's taking advantage of this crisis to meet his own ends," he said. "It seems demons have been given a free hand now."

As round-the-clock manufacturing of mountainous volumes of hand sanitizer and blue felt masks began, and quarantine mandates and shutdowns spread throughout America, I stayed very close to Krista. We prayed together at night and discussed how we would work past the interruption of the Mass and sacraments. We agreed to unite on Sunday through spiritual reading, meditative prayer, and serving the kids—Gabby had phoned to tell us Ole Miss was closing down. Sean and Shannon were dismissed from their schools.

But the ice felt thin. I didn't care about the virus; it was Krista who I feared would fall into the black waters, where my family would soon be sucked down with her.

Nine days had passed since Cardinal Gregory's announcement when I received a text message from Father Flum on Saturday, March 21: *Meeting tomorrow at 2 P.M. Bring Krista.* (Included in his text was an address and the name of an unfamiliar town.)

The following day, I took a left-hand turn onto a narrow road that split a field of corn. An abandoned tobacco barn in disrepair leaned into rows of corn on the right side of the road. I remember the day had the feel of springtime baseball; the air crackled under the big blue sky that covered a world frozen in fear. On the left was an old baseball field tucked behind a cornfield.

We took another left at an arrow and drove slowly down a country road with a few homes set off to the right. As gravel popped beneath my car's tires, we found ourselves beneath a thick mantle of low-lying branches from flowered trees. When I eased past the last branches on the road, a glistening large white estate thrust into view like a 3-D image. The home was framed by seemingly endless meadows. A two-horse barn was set off to the left, where chickens scratched the earth near their small pen. We had never before traveled to this part of Maryland.

Then I saw him. Father Flum stood far off on the porch, speaking with a woman. Springtime sunlight poured seeming floodlight onto his stiff violet fiddleback chasuble. It was the fourth Sunday of Lent when he turned to face Krista and me. He smiled through his Santa Claus beard.

There was a beat of silence before recognition and emotion passed through me like the miner startled by an overlooked gold-flecked streambed. Krista and I looked at one another, open-mouthed. I remember her glowing eyes. She remembers me shaking my head and laughing in disbelief. *This priest, this flare of hope, is going to celebrate Mass.*

I am unable to repeat in words what seemed sacred polyphony running through me at that moment. But if my soul had ordered and articulated it properly, it may have offered this: I was looking into the sacramental ontology of a priest *in persona Christi capitis*. Standing on the porch was a benevolent twenty-foot-tall Goliath of a priest pushing against the grain and waving in small assemblies of Lazaruses from the darkness. He beckoned the COVID- and world-wearied, the soul-parched, the nervous, the broken, and the left behind—and inoculated us with a single glorious word: *Come.* We walked to the porch, where Father Flum seemed to stand as a priest-titan from earlier times, as a great and sacred moonbeam of hope.

At the top step, he introduced us to the owner of the estate, a heavily accented elderly woman who had shared a long friendship with Pope Saint John Paul II. In the early 1980s, he had requested the vivacious and strikingly attractive woman to travel the world to fight for unborn children and against all forms of contraception. In short order, she whisked us downstairs and into her large basement, which was carved into a small bluff. We turned a corner at the bottom of the stairs and stepped through what seemed like a wardrobe's rear panel and into a different dimension. Krista and I were looking into the realm of the sacred and unmapped. It was one of the most stunning chapels we had ever seen. It seemed right away to us to be a catacomb that was overseen, prayed in, and guarded by a worker in the vineyard who'd built her life around service to God, promoting holy marriages and the child in the womb. It was in that small chapel where she daily adored Christ in the Real Presence, which had been "authorized" by a local bishop as repayment and reward for her vast spiritual work for tens of thousands of souls.

The walls of the chapel were covered in light-colored stone, which immediately brought visitors into a sepulchral, cave-like warmth. Inlayed into the walls were large pockets for old statuary, Bibles, and stained-glass windows, three of which filtered rays of afternoon light onto the small wooden altar. The largest of the hand-crafted windows carried an image of Saint Margaret Mary Alacoque in ecstasy—she has fallen to her knees at the foot of Jesus. Powerfully robed in cardinal red, Christ gestures for the French nun to look into His beating Sacred Heart. Hovering above, at the top of the window, is a purple-winged angel gripping a flowing scroll proclaiming: *Behold the heart that hath loved men so much.* Shoots of canary-yellow forsythia were choked in vases set on the sills of the stained glass.

To the right of the altar was a type of Tabernacle unseen in America. Seemingly birthed from the mind of an artisan from a different age, it was part gold and maroon and perched at the top of a stanchion of twisting ornamental mahogany wood that rose five feet off the hardwood floor of the altar. The large wooden crucifix, we were told later, had been hand-carved more than one hundred and fifty years ago by a Central American craftsman. Jesus hung from the Cross in guttural agony. The shoulder that bore the Cross was bloodied, His knees were torn. Veins, cartilage, and muscle still seemed to pulsate and shift from Christ's expired Body. His crowned head is dropped at an inconceivable angle.

A few other worshippers—there were nine in total— were praying on one of the two long wooden prie dieus at the front of the chapel. The kneelers were huge and seemed more designed for a cathedral, not a small and hidden-away place of prayer. The chapel was noiseless and soundproof, as if we had found a secret hatch by the Appian Way and climbed down.

In my imagination, I had melded with the portrait on my living room wall, joining the nineteen souls kneeling before the blessing hand of a young Irish countryside priest. Artist Aloysius O'Kelly's rendering of secret devotion, which he titled "Mass in a Connemara Cabin, 1833," was a cherished gift given to me by a merry priest, a seminary history instructor and distant relative who esteemed my uncle, Monsignor Wells. I had found myself looking into the portrait of the candlelit thatch-cottage Mass on count-less occasions, having intentionally positioned it on the wall directly across from where I prayed in the mornings.

Now, I was kneeling beside Krista in what seemed sub-terranean sacred grounds able to stop the hands of a clock. I praised God for hand-picking Father Flum as a seeming human fortress and caretaker of Krista's soul.

As I prayed in the silent chapel, I felt taken into the worn laborer's clothes of the hardy red-bearded Irishman in the portrait, who looked as if he had abandoned his work in the fields to attend the underground Mass. Many times I had imagined that farmer walking alone across lonely bogland, and risking the wrath and discovery of English landlords, to be fed by the Eucharist. Today, just for a single day, I was holding his hat in the time of famine, head bowed and kneeling to receive the priest's final blessing after the conclusion of the Station Mass. I was *the one* with the tousled hair, the man in the foreground on one knee, with his head inclined along with the eighteen other hungering souls. I was crammed into that cottage with the single small window, beneath the lantern and by the tattered portrait of the Sacred Heart. It was I breathing in the Irish incense of hearth-burnt peat floating in the darkening Connemara sky. Like that Irish farmer, I, too, had become the luckiest man on earth—for my Krista was being cared for, and loved, and even saved. As was I along with her.

Krista really knew for the first time that day that Father Flum would continue to stand by her in her time of recovery. Despite the evils that had been ushered in by the global pandemic, he would remain her human sustainer and safe port of call by offering the Sacrifice of the Mass. What she didn't know that afternoon was what Father Flum without a doubt did know: the Body and Blood of Christ were the curatives that would spiritually inebriate her eternal soul. "I knew I was being cared for in a special way that day," Krista told me last week when I asked her about that first Mass. "But I didn't know he was protecting me."

From the start of the COVID lockdown, Father Flum kept fastened to the burden of his identity. He wouldn't move one square inch from his duty to care for souls in time of a pandemic. I imagine some other faithful priests scattered throughout the globe found ways on that fourth week of Lent to feed their flock, but I sensed there were far more faithful priests—perhaps thousands—who struggled that Sunday while celebrating Mass alone. Father Flum, it seemed to me that day, came to us to administer the sacraments because he thought it would have been immoral and against God not to do so.

To illustrate his proposition, at this first Mass, he read the soaringly tender letter Saint Aloysius Gonzaga wrote to his mother while suffering the consequences of his choice to care for sixteenth-century plague victims. "He sees the plague as a chariot that's going to take him to Heaven," Father Flum said in his homily. "By his service to the poor, by expressing his Christian charity, he caught the plague. But it's going to take him to Heaven—and he's rejoicing in this. Essentially, he's saying, 'Rejoice, Mom, because you led me to this.'"

A chariot. Seemingly impervious to the crescendoing fear of death in the early spring of 2020, he took hold of the worldwide narrative and inverted it with a single word. An abrupt sense of reordering permeated the room. He proposed to the small congregation in a voice as soft as winter woodsmoke the paradoxical effect of the Coronavirus, suggesting that it offered us a potentially sacred gift if it was understood from a supernatural perspective. The virus offered us a ladder to climb to God rather than the *climbing down* action of the world into consuming thoughts of contraction of the virus. A new type of avarice had suddenly been birthed; the human body had become like gold. The sudden and immoderate attention it received had overpowered devotion to God, the sacred Mysteries, and one's own eternal soul.

In his first sermon, though, Father Flum flipped the script. *The virus is a potential mode of transport, the golden sleigh that could carry the plague-time saints and martyrs to Heaven.* That sleight of hand—the image of mystic ascent—managed to turn inside-out the very nature and function of disease. In a sense, the pandemic offered us a season of

hope—not despair—that quickened our thoughts of perhaps soon attaining eternity with God.

As the world's chorus belted out a dirge of panic, Father
Flum sang a sweet carol of hope into our souls. We would
attain peace during the pandemic, he said, only by considering eternity with God. The image of the chariot melted
into my soul that day like a poem, as a small flame of
new understanding. I imagine it did for the others as well.
He conceded that the virus gave reason for concern and
that survival instinct was natural and God-given. But he
said our emotions had to be harnessed and transformed
by grace. He encouraged us to strive to cleanse our hearts
and minds of fear at the latest COVID news and instead to
focus on making small acts of love to family members. The
incessant drumbeat of COVID-clamor was to be wholly
ignored, like the wise mom who pretends not to hear her
child's tantrum in a grocery store.

He offered examples of Saint Damien of Molokai's
immersion into the leper colony and Saint Francis of
Assisi's kiss of the leper. He said their behaviors were
simply supernatural choices of putting on the armor of
God to serve the love-starved. In the face of contracting
the diseases that could lead to their death, the two saints
unhesitatingly reached for the abandoned, diseased, and
stricken. When they considered the demand of love, he
said, they considered, not the diseased body in front of
them, but only its eternal soul. The saints, he said, lived
and acted with the mind of Jesus Christ, the Poor Man
of Nazareth who loved the poor. He encouraged us, that
throughout the pandemic, we should do the same. If we
viewed the virus through the eyes of the saints of Molokai
and Assisi—saints who lived with one foot on earth and
the other in Heaven—consideration of the virus would
soon recede. In time, if we firmed our resolve to surrender

to God our fears of contraction of the virus, then it would begin to seem inconsequential and even banal.

"The reality is that [life on earth] is not paradise. We're not staying here; we must live this life, every day of it, so that we might end up in the Father's House. That's what we're made for—we're made to live in the Father's House. So I would pray that, if any one of us—or all of us—get this illness and die, that through the intercession of Saint Aloysius Gonzaga we would have the same disposition he had in seeing our illness as a sort of chariot that would take us to the Father's House."

In the span of those few minutes, he had managed to capture and redirect us toward the dimension of the supernatural and infinite. He pointed us to the heroic way of Aloysius Gonzaga, who died too early in life while studying as a young Jesuit. This Italian young man was now an unmovable icon, a martyr of gallantry and tender love carved into our souls.

In addressing the indelicate reality of the Church-imposed sacramental moratorium, Father Flum reminded us that foremost we were to put our trust in God, not in the temporal responses of the Church. The Church offered the means to union with Christ, but not the end. For as long as the churches remained closed, he encouraged us to remain fixed on Christ—not on the sadness over the loss of the Mass and the sacramental plague. In a sense, he was telling us that we needed to build a cell within ourselves, a safe place in our soul to warm ourselves through friendship and frequent encounters with Christ throughout the days. If we daily stoked the fires of this small inner home through silent recollection, we would eventually find the pandemic to be little more than another event allowing us to attain oneness with God through prayer. But it would only serve as a reliable fortress during the pandemic shutdowns, he

said, if we made the decision to devote ourselves to meeting God as Christ did for Lent's forty days—or whatever
amount of days the pandemic hovered over our lives.

Meantime, he told us, in his humble way, that he would
do all he was permitted to help shepherd and provide for
us. He knew his priesthood demanded blood loyalty to
souls, especially at a time when fear and disorientation
were carpeting the earth. Those who were there that day
knew Father Flum would strive to elevate our souls to
God during the pandemic and time of sacramental loss.
Through many years of intense prayer, spiritual reading,
and hours of meditation in front of the Blessed Sacrament,
a kaleidoscope of images of Christ, Our Lady, and the
saints had grafted into his soul. We knew that in the ensu-
ing days, he would reach in to share his cornucopia with
us. It was the sacred bouquet of Christ, Our Lady, and the
saints that he knew would instill peace in us at a time when
it was hard to find.

It could not be seen, of course, but I imagine nervy
Mass-goers that day exhaled in orchestral unison. Unseen
tensions dropped to the chapel floor like absolved sin.
Standing before us was an unblinking priest of God, a pil-
lar who had just demonstrated a measure and meaning of
a shepherd.

In a personal way, that Sunday also marked the first day
of his becoming an abiding presence for Krista and me,
together as one, as she was still in the midst of freeing herself from the attacking shame and wounds inflicted thereafter. Perhaps pity prompted him to make room for us at
the secret Mass. Regardless, he told us later that day that
an unbreakable love and solidarity needed to be forged
in us. He believed, as I did, demons would work at warp
speed to press ruthlessly harder into Krista's wounds without access to what was acting for her as sacral medicines.

Without daily Mass and time in Adoration, she would be weakened and wide open for attack.

As folks left that day with the image of a chariot rising through the moonlight, I was, of course, thinking more of Krista and what the future would bring. As we drove home, I had never felt as matrimonially bonded with her; but I also understood the fragility and unreliability of emotions.

Chapter 12

Tethering Man to God

In the springtime of 2020, Father Flum and his tiny staff
were set to spill out onto country roads like old-timey
walking evangelists. Over the winter, they had planned
out a door-to-door springtime campaign of invitation to
attend Masses at Saint Michael's.

As news of the spreading virus in Europe began to creep
onto the nightly news, the staff disappointingly considered
putting their plans on hold. No one then, of course, knew
of the impending sacramental blackout.

Parish secretary Suzanne Stuart still remembers the day
Father Flum took the archdiocesan closure announcement
into his office and closed the door. Surrounded by many
dozens of books on canon law, sacred tradition, Catholic
encyclopedias, and magisterial teaching, he began to pray.
Thereafter, he began to read and reread the archdiocesan-
wide email and carefully delineate the distinctions between
guidelines and directives and law and spirit.

A few hours later, he opened his door.

The priest who by his nature and comportment often
kept his emotions in check, was beaming, with an expression perhaps similar to his look of delight after pinning
a superior opponent while wrestling for Good Counsel
High School in Silver Spring, Maryland. The time of study
of the directives in his office had uncovered thin fault

lines and small openings that allowed him—in narrower ways—to provide for and feed his flock sacramentally.

"It was that monk-like smile of his. He was looking down, but you could still see it behind his beard, the smile where you knew something really good was about to be shared," Suzanne said in her charming Southern accent. "He looked up at us and said, 'We're going to have Adoration. We're going to open things up.' And you could see his joy and excitement. He was going to bring folks to Jesus.

"On that first day of cancellations, it was like he said, 'If things are working to shut down Jesus, we're going to find ways to keep things open. People need a church to pray in,'" Suzanne said. "If people stop by to pray before work," he said to staff at the time, "I'm not going to throw them out."

Time never hung heavy in Father Flum's hands. He told his staff to prepare for Adoration seven days a week, from 8 A.M. to 9 P.M., which would begin the following day. No one knew at that moment how a parish of approximately 300 would congeal to adore Jesus Christ thirteen hours a day, seven days a week. The mathematics didn't work. The added challenge was that individuals worldwide were just beginning to fear contracting the virus and were bunkering indoors. In faith, though, the staff felt coverage would come because their pastor believed it would.

"Really, Father Flum had to be talked out of starting perpetual adoration," Suzanne said. "He never doubted we would cover each of the hours."

Within an hour of Father Flum's announcement to the staff, they began picking up the phone and sending out personal emails of invitation to adore Christ at Saint Michael's and letting them know the doors to the parish would continue to be open for them. The staff posted notices around the parish and created sign-up sheets. Father Flum told Suzanne that day he was refashioning her secretarial duties; her main job now was twofold: to be a herald of the glad tidings of Saint Michael's Adoration and to do her best to bring folks before the monstrance. In the meantime, because he had little else to do, he would begin to adore.

"We had a lot of gaps in coverage in those early days," Suzanne said. "But Father Flum covered them all. He was in there as many as six or seven hours a day, almost like he was beginning to live in front of Jesus. I remember walking in to pray at an uncovered hour and sometimes I'd see him asleep. Sometimes, I saw him fully prostrate in prayer."

Father Flum barely knew his future secretary when her husband, Scott, drowned in 2015. His entire family had been picnicking by a lake when his heart suddenly gave out while swimming.

At the wake, Father Flum waited in a long receiving line to mention a single thing to her: "Whatever you need, call me." Three days later, with a house full of stunned children who adored their dad, Suzanne felt her life falling apart. She picked up the phone, and Father Flum warmly invited her over to meet. He encouraged her to begin to pray the Divine Chaplet each day for a year for Scott's soul.

"He knew I needed something then, like an assignment to help me get Scott to Heaven and to help me through my pain. He was the only man outside of my husband that I trusted with my soul."

So, five years later, Suzanne was all in on letting folks know that Jesus was there for them at Saint Michael's.

Father Flum's love for Jesus at Adoration was raw from his earliest days at Theological College in Washington, D.C., in the 1990s. The seminary didn't offer opportunities to adore, so most nights he left his fellow classmates and drove from the seminary parking lot to the few parishes in the Archdiocese of Washington he knew offered Adoration. Most evenings, he headed twelve miles north, where he crossed the D.C. border and parked his car at Saint Mark the Evangelist in Adelphi, Maryland, which offered a humble perpetual Adoration chapel. For the young seminarian, the small brick-covered room attached to the rectory offered the sacred space and surfeit of light of Chartres Cathedral. There, he could adore Jesus for as long as time allowed. Some nights, Father Flum brought along a younger seminarian, who he had learned also had a devotion to the Eucharist.

"Father Flum invited me into his world, but really, it was an invitation to look into his soul," the man remembered twenty-six years later. "I was awakened to something I didn't know. He was far ahead in the game. I saw a seminarian who didn't just want to be a holy priest; even then I knew I was looking at a man who wanted to become a saint. I remember driving over with him; he'd have one hand on the stick shift and a Rosary in the other. We always prepared by praying the Rosary.

"When we walked in, he became riveted. I was adoring Jesus, but I was also watching him stare into the Host. It was a serene look, but I also saw the intensity of pure love. It was clearly not a Rule he was following or some overly pious way. There were no dramatics. I saw him then like a special-ops guy. His devotion was a profound love; it was alluring. I wanted what he had.

"One night, we were there late, and the next adorer didn't show up. For some reason, no one ended up coming, so we never left. For him, it was never a question; we were remaining with Jesus that night. So we made the all-night vigil and rolled into TC [Theological College] the next morning for morning prayer.... I could see that he was already working to gain mastery over himself. He was working to eliminate anything that would get in the way of giving himself to God. I didn't know it then, but he was already beginning to live the eremitical life."

It wasn't just Holy Hours at Saint Michael's then in those early pandemic days. Something else was happening. When, across the street, the strutting peacocks began their predawn shrieks and early rays of light stretched across pastureland, Father Flum began celebrating his private Mass with the back door unlocked.

When it came to priestly acts of love, he spurned every temptation to play it safe. In those first hours of what would become a long sacramental hinterland—public Masses without restrictions wouldn't be restored for more than a year in Washington—Father Flum made the choice to be unsparing in his love for his dispersed flock. He understood that a selection of the hardworking faithful would want to kneel before Christ in the Tabernacle before taking off for work.

If, on their way to work, unwitting folks pulled into Saint Michael's to pray—and he was in the midst of celebrating the Sacrifice of the Mass—well, perhaps the spiritual confluence of the timing was providential. It became the sacred secret of Baden, Maryland. Only a few folks knew. Thereafter, though, that small group began to filter in each morning for what seemed to them to be the only Mass on the face of the earth.

For Father Flum, heeding the Church was an absolute. "He always stressed to us the importance of obedience," his old classmate remembered. "He used always to say, 'We need to stay completely in line with the Chair of Peter.' He is a brilliant man, and he studied canon law extensively. He knew it inside and out."

Few knew about the private Mass. But Krista and I became aware of it, and joy flooded us.

In those early days, we rose from bed at 5:15 A.M., hurriedly dressed, and were out of the house by 5:30 for the forty-minute drive through the back roads to Maryland. Croom Road, the hilly two-lane country road, became what began to feel like an elixir poured into our souls. As the rising sun poked through the awning of trees, we wound our way past old tobacco barns and pastureland and humble homes with welcoming front porches and American flags. By the railroad crossing near where Croom meets Croom Station Road was our "dream home," a historic black-shuttered colonial that seemed to sleep in a state of regal grace in the soft morning light. It stood proudly on a small bluff, elegantly hemmed in by a white picket fence and towering elm trees. Two horses were usually just waking up to birdsong in the two-stall barn behind the home. As Krista and I admired the old home with corbelled brick chimneys, I often imagined falling asleep in an upstairs bedroom to the smell of chimney smoke and the sound of slow-moving trains at night. The home was an idyllic image of bygone warmth and order and spoke to me of Mary's home in Ephesus and a small house on a prairie. As we passed by, the home sang a private message of hope in me. During the darkest days, I had imagined such a home, where Krista, the kids, and I lived in harmony and peaceful order.

From there, we drove up a hill where we passed Moore's Country Store, some old Protestant churches, and daffodil-flecked sprawling farmland. Men in slow-moving pick-up trucks moved past us, heading west into the plague-seared nation's capital for construction work. After seventeen years of carving a similar path into the city, I remembered passing them and thinking I was the luckiest man in the world. They were headed into the belly of swallowing Washington, D.C., and I to an angel of a priest who mercifully kept open his church door.

The speed limit sign said 40 as we passed C&K Crabs, but I was usually driving 55 because we were getting closer. Father Flum started praying the Rosary at around 6:35 A.M., and it was our goal to arrive before he knelt on the floor in the rear of the church to announce the first mystery. He prayed the Rosary like a hidden Carthusian monk, his head bowed and mind filled with tender considerations of his Queen. Father Flum had a singular love for and fidelity to Our Lady and her Immaculate Heart. When he spoke of her in private conversations, his voice often softened and took on a different tone and rhythm. He sometimes looked past you into the distance, as if he were swept into a private joy of reverie and devotion.

He believed that Mary's intellect, because it hadn't been tainted by original sin, was far superior to that of any person ever born, save her Son. No one, not Thomas Aquinas, Augustine, any Church Doctor, Albert Einstein, or any secular intellect—even the angels—approached what her mind contained. "Because she was never marred by sin, her capacity for thought and wisdom was never dulled. Her wisdom and intellect were on a level we cannot understand. It transcended the world."

Those who were close to Father Flum knew he carried the Mother of God in his thoughts wherever he went. Once, I accompanied him into the home of a man dying in the middle of his living room. Aggressive brain cancer had rendered treatment useless, so his family agreed to set up hospice care at his home. He was trapped often within a noncommunicative haze, and his wife had watched him move from a state of fearfulness to anger and, finally, to depression. Saddled by disease and strong medication, his usual lighthearted manner and sunny personality had occasionally turned spiteful and accusatory, helping to push what once was a warm home into what seemed a place cloaked in a wave of shadows. Due to the gloom, his children had grown ill at ease, and a creeping detachment and discomfort with Dad began to take root.

Father Flum, who had been asked to anoint the man, did not know him or his family.

After entering the home, he moved directly to the man, who was incapacitated. He bent down and began softly to sing a lullaby into his ear, the *Ave Maria* in Latin. For a long while, in a house reshaped by the shadow of death, Father Flum's intention seemed to be to sing Mary directly into the man's soul through the portal of the ancient language. To me that day, he seemed to want to gather neatly from his own heart and soul his intense love for Mary and breathe it past the man's incapacitation, dulled senses, and even past the advanced stages of cancer—where his terror might be melodically and medicinally soothed. As his ode to the Queen filled the space, family members buried their heads in each other's shoulders.

As he sang the *Ave*, he began to anoint the man's head, where the cancer had settled. Suddenly, the man, who had been sedentary throughout, abruptly opened his eyes, threw out his arm, and grabbed the priest's wrist. His startled wife responded by attempting to pull her husband's hand away, but Father Flum gently said, *No.* He explained that anointings sometimes became physically painful. Her husband, he encouraged her, needed to endure it.

A minute later, the man emitted a startlingly loud exhaling sound, as if just freed from being trapped beneath water. Because the guttural release was the only noise he'd made to that point, it jolted all of us. Thereafter, the man trained his eyes on the priest. The haze behind his noncommunicative stare seemed to break apart, lift, and suddenly become replaced by a soft glow. In a hauntingly beautiful phenomenon, he seemed to take upon himself the gentle facial manifestations of the priest; like mirrors facing each other. A preternatural peace seemed to spread throughout the room. Family members were overcome with emotion by this sudden unveiling of angelic countenance.

I was sharing my observations with Father Flum later when he told me that the man's full-throated exhale was common during his anointings. He called it the "final release" or the "final reconciliation," "where all the fear of dying, pain from past sins, anxiety, and anger are finally let go from the inside and surrendered fully to God."

What lingers still in my mind in his administration of the Sacrament of the Sick was Father Flum's impulse to bring Mary immediately into the poor man's ravaged body. Those close to Father Flum knew the signature of his priesthood had been written by Mary, almost as if it was Our Lady—not his bishop—who had ordained him and sent him off as a priest. It was Mary who was enthroned in his soul, an echoing reminder that pointed him to her Son expired on the Cross and saying: *Now, Martin, you go do the same as a priest.*

On that first day, we opened the first set of doors and felt the morning chill collide with the cradling warmth of the country chapel. After passing beneath what seemed then a protecting bronze statue of the demon-hunter Saint Michael the Archangel, we opened the second set of doors. As the church doors closed behind us, we saw a small orb of light cast on a golden monstrance in the darkened space in front of us. We didn't know Christ in the Sacred Host was already there. We dropped to our knees, where peace swallowed us. It was as quiet as midnight in Bethlehem.

Sheltered by the soft glow of candlelight, the monstrance seemed to stand in the center of the altar as the last monstrance in the world. It was a magnetic vessel of *pulling* moonbeams, intent to gather us away from the thoughts of the corporeal and draw us into the sacred bosom of Christ. A small child with a supernatural sense for things would have seen within the monstrance the benevolent smile of the eternal man on the moon.

While the Host pulled us to Him, divine rays also pulsated out. The circumference of the monstrance was bordered by dozens of sharp-edged sun rays that burst like solar flares of the whispered reminder to a COVID-charred world: *I am* the world's medicine.

It was this message that Father Flum chose to present to his little flock before daybreak. This is the manner in which he would love us because he knew of God's impulse to lavish love upon His children in times of confusion and fear. He rose from sleep to expose God's ultimate gift of His Son. Father Flum knew the provision of time in Adoration was the greatest gift he could give his flock. Wide windows of time with Christ would be better, in a sense, than if he had crawled into the scrubs of a modern Jonas Salk and emerged from a lab with a COVID cure.

Saint Michael's was Molokai then.

The country church seemed to be a world-forgotten island, a safe place to tie up to the eternal Godhead-turned-leper. Saint Michael's was a safe port for those who pushed off that morning from the shoreline of a seemingly unraveling society. It seemed to me that day that a man in a worn cassock held a lantern from a small dock beckoning folks in to love the shunned Leper who had been abandoned in tens of thousands of Tabernacles throughout the world. Father Flum was Damien of Molokai then. His parish was the ribbon of sand and pinhole of hope amid countless archipelagos of locked churches, whose sheer cliff faces and impassable rock-strewn outcroppings pushed laity back out to sea.

Father Flum keenly understood what each of the Church's plague-time priests understood: *Jesus was the treatment and cure.* The Son of God, he knew, merged supernaturally into bloodstreams through the Eucharist, but also served travailed and sick souls as a balm and tonic during plagues. Although the Divine Physician and sacred remedy were left behind locked doors—he would be hoisted high in the monstrance at Saint Michael's.

Certainly, COVID-19 was a protagonist that understandably set the Church back on her heels in discerning a proper response—it had changed the face of the world overnight—but Father Flum regarded it as ephemeral and totally insubstantial when contrasted with eternity with God.

His allegiance and belief in the supernatural sank deeply into us that day. At a time when a worldly machine of government authorities and doctors was divinizing the human body in their heralding call to isolate, Father Flum tethered us to the Mystical. He knew time alone with Jesus in Adoration would direct us to where He already abided in our souls. In a fear-frozen world, Father Flum knew huddling us close to the warming furnace of the Eternal Truth would eventually work to incinerate the televised images of COVID-19 hot spots, death tickers, and humans who walked about covered in what resembled astronaut suits.

In seeing Father Flum that morning, we saw a Mediator for God gearing for a long battle. Horrifyingly, he watched muted spiritual leaders immediately cede Jesus to a worldwide political juggernaut, allowing Him to be peeled away by secular functionaries. In his crestfallen state, he became inflamed with love for Christ and His unsettled flock.

So, his parish grounds became Molokai, where the Leper in the monstrance would be tenderly watched over and kept company. Elsewhere, Christ in the form of the Leper was left forsaken, whereas at Saint Michael's, He would be adored nearly round-the-clock. If the Sacrifice of the Mass were going to be deactivated, he would find ways to pour Him as God's Blood into souls.

On that first day, we saw Father Flum off to the right in the front of the church, seated on a pew with his head and body curled over Psalms in the pages of his breviary. Krista led us to the front left side of the church, where she moved into a pew directly in front of the statue of Mary. It was on that morning she began to pray without a kneeler. In the weeks and months that followed, she would kneel on hard floors throughout an hour of Adoration, during Rosaries, and at the Mass. It was an unspoken gesture of mortification and penance for her binge drinking.

Although it was Lent, the atmosphere seemed more to me like Advent. The mood that morning carried heightened anticipation. The church was dark and still, like the darkness of Bethlehem soon to be filled with radiant Light. Like the traveling stargazers and shepherds, some of us traveled distances to encounter Jesus that morning.

At just past 6:30, Father Flum walked back toward the back of his church and knelt on the floor to lead the small body of worshippers in the Rosary, where he seemed to be a shepherd guarding his flock from the rear. I didn't know then that he chose the position near the vestibule to observe the number of people who would be entering. Tethered to obedience, he felt compelled to allow only a certain number of people to gather.

After the *Salve Regina*, he led prayers to Saint Michael the Archangel and Saint Joseph before walking to the front of the church to repose the Eucharist and disappear into his sacristy, where something gladiatorial began to unfold. His acolyte, Dave Mason, saw the inner fires of Father Flum slowly become stoked each morning. He still pauses and falls temporarily wordless when recalling those ten minutes before the start of Mass when he saw a priest's soul slowly become aflame. At a time when the public Mass had been barred throughout the world, Father Flum seemed to have traveled back in time into a cell and the skin of a desert monk preparing to celebrate his last Mass on earth. The sacristy then was an inner sanctum, as solemn and consequential as Gethsemane.

It became a silent and sacred waiting room, where a priest seemed to gird himself to disappear into the Holy Sacrifice of the Mass as it was celebrated in the pages of the Book of Revelation. It was like a transmutation of a man that Dave beheld each morning. Father Flum seemed to have passed into something incorporeal. The sacristy then was an antechamber where he seemed to become more spirit than flesh.

"It was like he was on a sortie against the world. I have no other words to describe what I saw," Dave said. "The sacristy held a deadly serious atmosphere. The feeling then was similar to being with my wife in the final moments of pregnancy, as we prepared to go to the hospital. The bond was strong, and words were spoken rarely and only when necessary. It was that same type of aura and intensity."

He washed his hands and asked God to remove the profanity of his flesh to prepare it to enter the sanctuary of the King of Kings. Then, one by one, beginning with the amice and alb, he solemnly mouthed his vesting prayers, as if he were whispering them into the ear of his Guardian Angel. These weren't the pre-Mass rubrics of a hyper-pious cleric—they were the time-honored traditions, gestures, and deliberate manner of a humble man girding himself with spiritual armor. When the acolyte stole glances at Father Flum during his vesting prayers, he saw the incandescence of a priest unhurriedly and noiselessly setting himself right in order to enthrone Jesus within his heart.

"I saw a man then as *alter Christus*; he seemed to be readying himself to do something not of this world," said Dave, a married father of six children. "When he asked me at the start of the pandemic if I would assist him as his acolyte, he expressed to me—in a sincere and very serious way—that he expected total reverence and silence in the sacristy before each Mass. He told me that a priest who prepares to celebrate the Mass, when he vests and when he prays, needs silence ... and I saw as he prepared that his face was set and his demeanor seemed of a supernatural order."

In the sacristy, during the early stage of Coronavirus hysteria and Mass closures, Dave seemed to have stepped past a border wall and into an untraveled countryside. In Father Flum, he saw a priest slowly ripening himself to be made worthy of taking on the character of His Son.

The final pieces of the scaffold for the Mass were set when Father Flum slipped his rough-hewn fiddleback chasuble over his torso and wordlessly eyed Dave over to join him in prayer. It was in those moments the space behind the altar seemed to become bathed in light, as if it contained something electric, like the tight space of the starting gate after Secretariat stepped in. They stood shoulder-to-shoulder before a large crucifix and oriented themselves for the Sacrifice of the Mass. After a short period of recollection, they began softly to pray aloud the elegiac text of Saint Thomas Aquinas' pre-Mass Declaration of Intention. As Dave listened to the ancient words ... *I come sick to the doctor of life, unclean to the fountain of mercy, blind to the radiance of eternal light ... wash away my defilement ... enlighten my blindness*—he felt he had trespassed into a medieval sanctum where Father Flum was anchoring himself to the burden of his identity and working to fill his lungs with the hymns of Bethlehem angels. Since the beginning of his priesthood, Father Flum knew the sacral Mysteries weren't of the natural order, so in his zeal for souls, he had prepared to celebrate the Mass by lifting his little flock into something liturgically beautiful and sacred, like a Mass prayed at the feet of God and His Son in Heaven.

Aquinas' ancient pre-Mass words emerged like puffs of incense rising into the lap of God. It was the sacred prayer of priest-saints. "He had invited me in to stand together with him against evil," Dave said. "He was about to bring Jesus to the people, and in a sense I had been asked by him to be his helper. It seemed he had asked me to help him prepare for war," Dave said. "When I began to see the depth of his priesthood and his deep love for God and souls, I thought back then that I would have left everything behind and followed him into war. If he had explained to me why it was necessary for my, or my wife's and children's and grandchildren's, salvation, I would have gone."

Krista and I, along with a handful of others, watched the sacristy door open, where Dave rang the bell that brought us to our feet. Father Flum gently closed the door of the sacristy and proceeded to the altar, where he genuflected to the Tabernacle and bent to kiss the altar. In a real way, at that kiss that began the Mass, Father Flum had unwittingly made of himself a vanguard of priestly identity and hope for the rocky road that lay ahead. If a comic strip bubble had settled above the altar at that moment, it may have proclaimed a single thing—*Now the darkness has lost its terror.*

As he processed to his presider's chair on the right side of the altar, I felt I had won the unwinnable lottery within a time of sacramental moratorium. A father had come to protect our one-flesh union and set it before the face of God. He had shown up to give us the world's exquisite and unsurpassable gift of the Mass.

Before he blessed himself, he very quickly scanned each face of the small gathering of worshippers, for whom he had always tried to provide uncalculated care. If your eyes were closed in prayer for those brief seconds and you didn't catch it, you missed out on a spiritual father's ineffable gaze of deep love. My soul melted into something warm and languorous when his eyes passed over Krista and me, as if we had suddenly been pulled into an inn's hearth fire on a cold winter night. That tender look began to peel back what often seemed interminable and unbeatable darkness. Krista's disconsolation and shame, hundreds of wearied bike-path walks, restless nights of worry for my children, and all the early-morning sweeps of my home all began to recede and lose their grip. It seemed God had hand-selected that cool March morning to respond to a decade of despairing prayers for order. The big-bearded priest on the altar was his answer, and I imagine a few demons were worried then.

I saw from the soft glow on his determined face he wanted to celebrate the Mass perfectly—not in a hyper-zealous or saccharine way—but in a manner that revealed he had been bound to perfection by God. He had been called to a higher code, and most of us knew that day he stood on the altar as the most prepared priest in the world. For years, he had prayed the Divine Office, often from a pew in his church where his visage frequently took on the visage of a Trappist monk in the valley of unreachable mountains. He had fasted, mortified his body and emotions, and surrendered each day of his priesthood to Mary, like a knight consecrating to her a lifelong vigil. The shine in his eyes revealed his heart; he stood that morning in the bosom of his ontological identity as the Slaughtered Lamb. We knew, if canon law had permitted it, he would have celebrated the Mass as often as someone requested it.

He stood at the altar before a disparate set of upper- and lower-middle-class worshippers, where whites merged with blacks, the young with the old, and the blue collared with the corporate. Each of us came as beggars who rose from sleep in darkness that morning seeking to become enfolded into the embrace of the sacred Mass.

When the Mass began, news reports on death counts, closures, and maps of COVID hot spots sprung up in worldwide cities like attacking schools of Amazonian red-bellied piranha. The world was on fire then, but Saint Michael's cast quiet light, like the invisible beams that warmed shepherds as they descended hillsides en route to the Bethlehem stable. As that morning's global COVID caterwaul was just cranking into gear for the day, the small parish was a hymn and benediction to the wholesomeness of old-country ways, where a hardy and quiet set of believers came to adore God and be fed by the supernatural protector hidden in a mostly diminished host.

At the Confiteor, he swung his right fist aggressively, a threefold thumping heard by congregants in the rear of the church. "I never saw him sin in any way," said Dave, who recalled the strikes echoing like a drum. "Maybe [others] noticed a venial sin or two, but I imagine the sins he regretted were committed and absolved a very long time ago."

When he approached the ambo to proclaim the Gospel, he pulled a chain to switch on a small light that spoke as a metaphor for our souls. He didn't bring prepared notes; he never did. His words that day are lost in an eddy of the numberless thousands of words that would follow over the next year and a half; words carved from caverns of his soul and brought to life as hermeneutics that would slash through the thickets of COVID distraction to bring to bear the incarnate Son of God. He was a carefully spoken man who stood powerfully behind the pulpit, where his precise diction, the gentle movement of his hands, and the reclamation of vanishing Catholic words—*vouchsafed, incandescent, clement, veiled*—were unpretentiously delivered. Although he always preached with assuredness, his sermons were often unobtrusive challenges for listeners to increase their love and devotion to God. His ultimate hope was for laity to encounter Christ and bring Him to every corner of their lives. He wanted his parishioners to live holy lives and to commit themselves to ongoing conversion of heart.

He was as manly and earthbound as any priest in America—not because he bent rebar, cleared brush, and split thousands of logs in his cassock—but because he seemed to preach as if he lived in an unseen space between Heaven and earth. Anchored to the wisdom of Church Doctors and theologians, his sermons often seemed pulled from ancient scrolls. His heart was filled with the images of Old Testament prophets, monks, and saints, who often served as the instructors of his sermons. The thrust of his pulpit work was to transform and convict listeners to become other christs. He spoke plainly about what God expected; He wanted us to become perfect as His Son was perfect. This was not a throw-away suggestion; He wanted us each day to strive to become canonized saints.

Everything about his preaching changed when he spoke of Our Lady, his muse and Mother of his soul. The cadence of his voice softened, and his face took on light. When he preached on Mary, he seemed to be speaking directly to her, as if she stood close to him at the altar. A penetrating depth settled in his eyes, and a mannered courtliness enveloped him, as if he were communing with the saints who also consecrated their lives to her. His most beautiful vestments carried images of Mary. When he preached on her Feast days, he seemed to catch fire. He always gazed into what seemed a middle space above the pews, like he was watching the flight of an eagle above treetops. The sea-change of his behavior wasn't pious theatrics; Father Flum was devoted to her Immaculate Heart. He had given her a free hand with his priesthood and entrusted to her his long fasts, daily hours of prayer, indignities, and loneliness—as kindling to allow him to speak well of her Son and to proclaim the coming Kingdom. He had made himself her slave.

He once told me: "She was the one who pulled me out of the trash heap. After that, I was going to do whatever she said. The thought of being a priest was an absurdity to me. But in the watershed moment of my life, Mary told me, 'I know *you're* not the right material, but my Son is going to accomplish his priesthood through you.' That's when I knew I had to become a priest. Mary gave me an intimacy with her Son that I didn't think was possible."

He rarely preached about what he called "the virus." He mostly dismissed it from his sermons as the latest inconvenient protagonist that troubled the hearts of his parishioners. In those early days, though, he did often use the virus to serve as robust teaching mechanisms. He said fear of dying was at its heart a lack of confidence in God, who had long ago conquered death. Throughout Lent and the Mass-darkened Easter season, he contrasted the everlasting joy of Heaven with the temporal calamity of fear, saying the most notorious apostates were those who broke from the grip of God because they feared their death. "They surrendered their faith to maintain their physical life," he said. "For a few more years here on earth, they traded their eternal soul." He was genuinely confused, and even saddened, by those who worried or spoke excessively about the virus. "Everything surrendered into the furnace of Jesus' Sacred Heart," he reminded us, "would bring about deep peace in you."

Father Flum knew his preaching was tantamount to illuminating souls and bringing them to a friendship with God and awareness of eternal Truths, but he held the Eucharistic Liturgy much higher in esteem. He would have agreed never to preach another word so long as he could confect the Eucharist. Where his preaching captivated hearts, his actions in the Eucharistic Liturgy transported souls. Mass-goers were taken into the heart of his identity, someone who brought Jesus into the natural world through the words of Consecration. When he spoke those words, the altar seemed to become a sacred countryside, a place where only monks and hermits are given passport.

As he celebrated the Mass *ad orientem*, he seemed to want to pry a COVID-consumed world away from the news and orient it back to our true home in Heaven, where we would look along with him into the East and the rising sun. Mass-goers couldn't see his countenance as he faced the Tabernacle, but he seemed to his acolyte to have become bathed in solemnity, knowing he held Jesus as a tiny child in his hands. He usually opted for the Roman Canon—the longest and most ancient Eucharistic Prayer. When he spoke the words of Christ's essence— "*this pure victim, this holy victim, this spotless victim*"—his voice became a plaintive, severe whisper. When he spoke the word "*spotless*," it came to his mouth like a tremor. That single descriptor seemed his *breathed* inner contrition for all of humanity for our slaughtering of the Pure Lamb through our treachery and sinfulness.

At the Epiclesis, before praying the words of Consecration, he began what seemed to his acolyte a tender systematic withdrawal from the altar and into the Upper Room. With raptness, he prayed the words of Jesus at the Last Supper as if he were standing and warming the hearts of twelve wide-eyed men. He bent low into his Sacramentary

for the Words of Institution and repeated the words—
"This is my Body," and "This is my Blood"—in a breathy
voice pulled from a mystic place in his soul. Because he
prayed the Mass *ad orientem*, Dave was the only one to
see his eyes riveted to the Host in what seemed a raw and
hypnotic trance.

On multiple occasions, almost daily for several weeks,
Dave knelt transfixed on that altar, as if he had seen a
ghost. He began to see movements of what seemed invisible adorers.

"I have to say something now about what used to happen on the altar. I am a man who's worked his entire life
with visible and solid things. So what I saw didn't initially
make sense to me," said Dave, who started as a driver for
a compressed gases company before working his way up
to become its vice president of operations. "But when he
stretched out his arms and elevated the host, I will tell you
that I often saw the floor start to ripple, like sheets that had
begun to flutter in the wind.

"This movement, this pulsating of the floor, happened
during the Consecration and at other times during the
Eucharistic prayers. It seemed to happen when he looked
into the high arches of the church as he extended his arms
with the Eucharist. When I saw him then, he seemed to be
looking into the face of God. His eyes, his face, his entire
being seemed to have lost all awareness of anything else;
like he was in a different place.... After about three weeks
of seeing these things move, I mentioned it to Father
Flum. He responded casually, and said hundreds of angels
were present on altars during this Consecration; he said
it was the same on altars all over the world. He told me
that I shouldn't be concerned about what I was seeing. He
encouraged me not to look for angels, but to stay focused
on what was actually happening on the altar, that Christ
had come into the form of bread.

"Those that know me know I am not one to *see* these types of things. But I do know this—what I saw was something not of the natural world. I have never seen anything like it.... I have never been so close to that measure and depth of that kind of love for the Eucharist. Maybe that's why the Holy Spirit and angels seemed to be all around at the Consecration."

Although the flowing tide of adoration remained hidden from my eyes, I was given something just as worthy. Seeming choirs of angels at that first Mass heralded a single thought into my mind: Krista's path of healing had been given a heartbeat. As she knelt peaceably beside me, I wasn't certain if my heart burned more because of the transcendence of the sacredness of the Mass, because of the mysterious self-emptying love of its presider—or because Krista's soul was astir and being gently sculpted beside me. It didn't matter, though, because I knew Krista was safe within the cocoon of the Mass that would be offered again the next morning, and the morning after that, and on and on. An image of those underground sunrise Masses comes to mind these years later: we had discovered a portal into a type of Milky Way, a place where the Eucharist came to life each morning as the birth of a new star and candles flickered like never-landing comets. I don't know what Krista felt then, but as I floated amid that soft and never-ending blanket of constellations, I felt pulled backward in time and into a hidden stone cottage where I pushed, elbow-to-elbow, into a room overflowing with cradled babies, peat-stained farmers, peasants, fishermen, and commoners—who had gathered as one flesh for the Sacrifice of the Mass in a Connemara glen British sentries never thought to check.

The virus didn't spread that morning: it never did at Saint Michael's in the months and years that followed.

Chapter 13

The Priest Who Stayed

In those early purgatorial months of the pandemic, Krista and I kept steering our car toward Croom Road and to the Mass at Saint Michael's that had become part of the abiding rhythm of our lives. It was on these early drives that something both charming and powerful slowly began to unfold—what we both noiselessly felt to be a momentous turn. Krista and I became like newlyweds again. We drove past our "dream home" by the railroad tracks and bore our souls about a future without secrets, shame, and ghosts. A slow-motion operation of grace opened on those country roads, where we began to love and speak to one another with no boundaries or agendas. The drives beneath brightening morning skies became some of the most purely happy days of our marriage. With the car radio always turned off, some spans of the drive were quiet. Unlike the polar hush we had known so well, this was a sacred silence, where I imagine we often internally thanked God for His providence and patience with us. When we prayed aloud on those farmland drives, it seemed we had stepped through an old fence line in the French countryside and into Millet's *Angelus* field of order.

One of the small treasures of attending Mass was Father Flum's gracious gift of providing parishioners with COVID-amnesia whenever we stepped into Saint Michael's for Mass or private prayer. From the beginning of COVID, holy water fonts were always filled to their rims. As other pastors, in order to prevent what they said could pose as a spreader of the virus, obliged bishops' motions to empty the small vessels, Father Flum viewed holy water in the opposite manner. He knew the blessed water was medicinal and actually would supernaturally ward off disease. He discussed masking at Mass just once, at the very beginning of the pandemic. "As a priest, one of my roles is not to be your babysitter," he said with a smile after the close of Mass. "You must make your own decision on whether you feel masking is necessary." At the Mass, he knew his role was to cohere the "masked and unmasked" together in their worship.

I imagine because of the dark night we had endured for so many years, Krista and I never considered the effects of what masking, hand gels, or keeping our fingers far from holy water fonts might do to protect our bodies. We were greedy for graces then and thought very little of our physical welfare beyond the healing of Krista's wounds. For the first time, we approached the Communion rail to receive the Eucharist side-by-side. For me—and I imagine for Krista as well—kneeling to receive Jesus together on our tongues held greater intimacy and romance than anything shared on our Tuscan honeymoon.

Perhaps because the sacred rhythm of these days was unlike anything we had experienced in our marriage, the Evil One's presence, remarkably, seemed to enlarge. At a point where Krista's soul had never been more full, she told me she often was pulled to miasmic reminders of her perceived worthlessness and shame, tempted to believe that those were places that God could neither reach nor repair. Mocking voices tore through her, often while she prayed, telling her she was Father Flum's little hypocrite.

Her Scarlet Letter was "F": God could never love a *fake* like her.

On a handful of nights, she succumbed to the voices.

Morning drives to Mass after these falls were tough. Krista kept her head down, guilt knifing into her. Even though I knew cooperation with grace took time, I drove like a heartbroken teenage boy blurred by emotions. Pulling into the parking lot of Saint Michael's those mornings felt like a long-distance runner's finish-line collapse.

Father Flum had prepared me for these dark moments, telling me to beg God for temperance and fortitude should Krista suddenly fall. "Krista is healing," he told me. "The Evil One knows it." He told me the work of overcoming my impatience after a fall would be the single hardest thing I would have to do—but he also said it was the greatest gift I could give Krista. "I can see the grace at work in Krista, and I know you can, too," he told me one day in the parking lot of Saint Michael's. "As her husband, you need to remember her movements toward healing and love her more on the hard days. She needs to know that you believe in her after her falls—and she'll know it by your calm and by the look in your eyes."

As I left the pew for the altar rail on those hard mornings, Krista stayed kneeling on the floor, head buried in her hands, where I imagine a fusion of ignominy and self-loathing flapped in her conscience like scattering families of bats. After Mass, she confessed her sin to Father Flum. As we drove home to face the day, we both gave way to the sacramental graces. The Eucharist, I prayed, would empower in me stalwart love for Krista throughout that day. For Krista, I imagine, she prayed that the grace of absolution would aid in stamping out her pyre of shame so that Christ's peace might rise from its embers. I imagine, too, she implored the aid of Mary, asking that she come to her while also requesting that she crush Satan's head.

One day Krista told me something startling. In spiritual direction, she confessed to Father Flum another fall. Since the beginning of the "COVID Masses," she had drunk three or four times over the course of the Pascaltide. As Father Flum worked to identify the triggers pulling her to still want to drink secretly, Krista remembers casting blame on me or some other issue at home. After some back-and-forth, he spoke with a frankness to which Krista wasn't accustomed. As if pulling apart heavy drapes in a sunless part of her conscience, he told her, "I think it's gotten to a place where your love for the demon in you is more powerful than anything I can do for you," he said.

She was cut to the bone. After a few moments of registering his diagnosis, Krista weakly asked him to explain what he meant.

Father Flum looked her in the eye and said in a plain and un-nuanced way, with a sliver of exasperation. "You continue on a path that is taking your soul to Hell."

Krista shriveled into herself and stayed quiet.

After a period where neither spoke and only the ticking of his office clock on the wall could be heard, she opened his door and zombied out of the rectory, across the empty parking lot, and into the church, where a woman was praying in the second pew before the monstrance. She knelt in front of the statue of Mary, whose Immaculate Heart suddenly seemed to have closed up as she knelt dazed before her. When the shock to her soul gave way to tears, Krista felt her body shake. She had the awareness to walk back into the cry room, where she shut the door and prayed in tears for Mary to intercede. But after some time, she felt the part of the dying soldier on a battlefield, who cries out for his mother who he knows won't come.

After gathering herself, she steeled herself and walked back into Father Flum's rectory. Because Krista knew him well, she understood he wouldn't be moved by her emotions. She handed him a carton of eggs from the chickens we had begun to raise to keep Shannon active while COVID kept her from school. Father Flum thanked her, his mood unchanged.

She drove home with her head on fire, fixated on two thoughts: the immensity of her eternal soul and perhaps having lost the shepherd who was trying to save it.

I am not certain if the dreary news Krista shared with me about her meeting with Father Flum could have come at a worse time. I had just agreed to write the biography of Venerable Aloysius Schwartz, an American priest on the path to canonization, and was set to depart later that week to the Mexican Girlstown and Boystown communities he had founded in the wake of the Korean War. I felt I had to go. With six months to complete the manuscript, some nuns from the Sisters of Mary religious Order he founded, who cared for "Father Al" as he was dying from Lou Gehrig's disease in the early 1990s, would help to get me started on my writing. I scheduled a three-week trip, which other than her time at the rehabilitation center, would be the longest period of time Krista and I had ever been apart.

For the first time, Krista spoke to me of her long habits of drinking that were possibly leading to her damnation. I was speechless. She surprised me by asking if I shared Father Flum's sentiment that love for her "demon" surpassed anything else in her life. In the silence of formulating a response to the most remarkable question she had ever asked me, I suddenly thought of the thick coffee table book, *Compendium of the Miraculous*, I had recently purchased. Its author, Albert Graham, had spent more than twenty years researching and writing about Church-approved apparitions, divine revelations, mystical phenomena, locutions, near-death experiences, and the like.

One section of the book in particular—saints' and mystics' graphic visions of souls in Purgatory—gained the attention of several of my friends at a recent men's retreat. Graham wrote of Saint Frances of Rome, who told her spiritual adviser of being taken to Purgatory by her celestial angel. She was given a glimpse into an "underground prison of boiling oil and pitch" filled with writhing and burning souls. At a lower level of Purgatory, she saw souls "struggling not to drown in what appeared to be a pond filled by liquified metal." Other saints—including Lydwina de Schiedam and Maria Maddalena de' Pazzi—were given similarly horrifying visions of what seemed to be a realm worse than Hell.

It struck me at that moment to find the book. I asked Krista to wait for a minute as I left for the bookshelf in our bedroom.

I opened the book and explained what had shaken my friends and me on retreat. I read some of the saint's visions of Purgatory and then thumbed through other sections of the book—which was lavished with old Catholic portraits and sacred art. Together, for a while, we read about saints—Teresa of Ávila, John Bosco, Faustina Kowalska, Bernardine of Siena, and others—who were given intoxicating visions of Heaven.

"Krista, Father Flum isn't telling you that you are going to Hell," I said. "He is asking you to avoid it by turning everything over to God. I'm in the exact predicament that you are. Unless I repent of my sins and turn away from my bad habits, my soul's in jeopardy."

In the sea of our emotions, we agreed we needed to fight harder to surrender to God to save us. We also discussed what to do about what Father Flum had told her. His remarks about her path to Hell and hidden love affair with a demon were unsparing. Although I imagined his directness came in a moment of exasperation, I also knew he was plainspoken about the consequences of repeated sin. For him, directness was simply a more intense condition of his fatherly love.

One thing I knew, though, that day: he had scared Krista straight—or at least he did for that moment in time. As Our Lady of Fátima had done for the three shepherd children, he had seemingly opened the earth to allow Krista an image of her soul burning in Hell.

As Krista and I discussed our lives and eternal souls, it struck me that Father Flum had become the most important person in our lives. At a time when Americans had riveted their gaze to flat screens for the latest word from cable news anchors, Anthony Fauci, or some unknown man standing on a stage in front of World Health Organization logos, I continually found myself thanking God for answering the dim constellation of my prayers for Krista's healing by sending Father Flum. He had been helping my family in so many ways before the pandemic, but now—within the void of the sacramental blackout—he had cooperated with the Holy Spirit to save Krista. He was a torchlight, the spiritual progenitor who returned, again and again, to roam about her cave to light the way out. He had sacrificed an untold number of hours to save a single soul.

For the same reason, Krista and I slept restlessly that night. Krista wanted to tell Father Flum the following day that she needed him in her life. And if I got the chance, I wanted to tell him the same thing.

We drove to Saint Michael's the next morning speaking few words. Krista entered the confessional after Mass, and Father spoke plainly, as he had done the day before. This is how she remembers the conversation unfolding.

"I need you," she said. "to stick with me."

"I need you," he said. "to remain close to Jesus."

"Tell me what to do," she said. "I don't want this anymore. I'm exhausted with the shame and way I'm living. I know what it's doing to my family."

Krista said the confessional turned quiet as Father Flum seemed to have entered into a daydream, as if he were listening to a secret thought. He sat crouched over with his forearms resting on his thighs, his thin and faded purple stole loosely dangling. After some time, he rose and looked at Krista with eyes that had taken on the holy love of Christ's when he looked at Peter at the moment of his final denial. "Krista, Jesus wants you very close to His Sacred Heart," he said. "He loves you as His special daughter, and He wants you near Him so He can heal you."

Krista's eyes welled. In shame, she still mostly only felt Christ's continual disappointment with her. At this point of her renewal, she still often felt hated by God.

"There is no better place and nothing better you can do now than spend time with Jesus at Adoration," he said. "He will strengthen your will and reveal His love. Little by little, in time, you'll begin to feel yourself being pulled into the furnace of His love. He wants nothing more from you now than spending time close to His Sacred Heart."

"I know," Krista said through tears. "He's with me in Adoration, but I can't feel Him with me, and I can't hear Him."

"Well, Krista, that's why I'm suggesting you spend more time with Him. As you heal now, Jesus wants you even closer to Him," he said with a warm smile. "And He is healing you from your shame. Kevin and your kids see it. I see it, but until you see the depth of His love for you as His spiritual daughter, your healing will only advance so far."

After a period of silence, he came up from his hunched position and said what seemed to have been placed into his heart. "Until you hear Christ begin to speak to you, I want you to spend your time at Adoration praying to Our Lady," he said. "Spend time resting quietly in her Immaculate Heart. When you speak with her, ask her to reveal her Son to you."

Krista brightened. For years, it was Mary who she felt had been maternally protecting her during dark moments.

Thereafter, they spoke about a spiritual plan for each day that Krista said she would follow. The lion's share of the plan involved increased hours of Adoration and an offering of the commonplace routines of home life—errands, chores, and conversations—as hour-by-hour consecrations to God. These small offerings to God of the minutiae of the day, he suggested, hallowed the home and made it a place of harmony and right order.

The night before I left for Mexico, Father Flum drove out to our home, where Krista prepared a huge bowl of shrimp Fra Diavolo, with cheese trays, garlic bread, and homemade cannolis. It was a spark of joy to see him engage with my family, where he seemed to trade stories and laugh with them as a visiting uncle, and not a faithful Catholic priest. After sitting around the dining room table for a few hours, the kids retreated to their bedrooms.

As we sat alone, he asked us to lead him to all the places in our home where Krista hid bottles and secretly drank. As we entered each of the rooms, closets, and secret places, he scattered blessed salt and holy water and whispered prayers I couldn't understand. Before leaving, he gathered Krista and me by the kitchen island and prayed a long exorcism prayer of authority. I felt in those moments, as I stood close to Krista in the mysterious space, the indestructible presence of Christ and untamed holy angels among us.

As we walked Father Flum to the door, I knew—and perhaps Krista did as well—that the warmth, laughter, and grace of the evening were the actualization of the failed night from four years earlier when the long-bearded healer of souls couldn't get through the front door. I walked him to his truck alone on the pleasant late spring night. Before getting into his truck, he told me that all was going to be well, and for the first time, I believed it. When I boarded a plane early the next morning, hardly another soul was on it.

While I was away, Krista began to spend as many as three hours a day at Adoration. She would sometimes text me at night to say the hours often passed by like minutes.

I would text back. *Minutes? Come on!*

Yes. I'm not being a pious drama queen. It's what's happening.

She was praying the Rosary unhurriedly, always with her eyes closed, where in each decade she placed herself as close to Mary as she was able. She told me she rarely brought in spiritual reading or even the Bible. She preferred to spend time in meditative silence, where, she told me, she had found peace despite still feeling outside of Christ's covering embrace. Father Flum assured her that as intimacy with Mary surged, Jesus would begin to split apart her wounds and open self-awareness of His love for her as His daughter. Once she fully surrendered her uncertainties about His love—and all the dark habits that had for years filled that void—she would become the beggars, the crippled, Magdalens, Matthews, and betraying Peters who lived again. He would leave no part of her barrenness untouched by His grace. His grace, Father Flum explained to her, would cast light into her pain and unknowingness to make plain finally the goodness of her heart.

On some days, Father Flum quietly walked up to her in the pew. "Keep doing what you're doing," he whispered before beginning his own prayer. "Stay in that place."

When Krista was at home with the kids, she worked to keep them upbeat in the midst of college and school closures. Zoom classes had grown stale for each of them. Although the world remained in a seeming freefall of fear around the midpoint of 2020, no one in our home seemed even to think about the virus.

When I returned from Mexico, Krista had a glow I had never seen. Her eyes were clear and her face carried a shine and brightness. Charmingly, she didn't even know it. A few days after I arrived home, Krista arranged for us to pick strawberries along with Gabby, Shannon, and a friend. When I looked at the photographs of the day later that evening, Krista looked radiant, seemingly having aged many years in reverse. At night, we kept the mutinous strains of the COVID-saturated televised news turned off and settled in the living room, where Krista sipped from hot mugs of maple-flavored tea and read a book from a stack of thin Jacques Philippe books. I recall sitting across from her with Rome's 900-plus-page *Positio* in my lap. The enormous hardback compendium contained the documentation supporting Aloysius Schwartz's cause for being promoted to the title of Venerable in the Church. In silence, I periodically looked up from a page and saw a woman who seemed to have been incandescently transformed. The room was bathed in quiet, and the order of the old coastal town of Ephesus often came to mind.

I spent most of my days writing. Krista spent hers with the kids and running errands after Mass and Adoration. She was beginning to establish some close friendships with women at Saint Michael's. Usually, at some point in the day, she came into my office and sat on the chair to my left, where she quietly read. Sometimes, she set her book on her lap and asked if she could share what had moved her heart earlier at Holy Hour or in the Mass. As she shyly spoke of her inner movements, Krista had unwittingly given me the writer's greatest gift: she had become my muse, the motivating force and wellspring of my words. The rumbling dark storm that had settled behind her eyes for years had been pushed out to a great settled sea of peace. I looked into her shining eyes as she shared nakedly her convictions to renounce and flee her past and center her life under the wing of Christ. The tinniness or hollowed-out promises of first fervor were no longer there. I was looking at a soul in the process of being elegantly refashioned by God, and as I sat at my desk, I felt we, at last, had set foot in Cana.

Chapter 14

Darkness and Light

Shannon's school reopened in the early fall, so I stopped joining Krista for early-morning drives to Saint Michael's. Because daily Mass and Adoration had become the peaceful pattern of her life, I volunteered to help get Shannon ready in the morning and handle carpools twice a week. Krista fell into the habit of daily texting me Father Flum's homilies, which she had recorded on her cell phone, for me to listen to on my thirty-minute drive home from Shannon's school. There were mornings when I felt what seemed to be a sudden chemical dopamine rush of thoughts and images. I knew as I listened to that day's sermon that the darkness in Krista's soul was being invisibly carved out in a methodical fashion by the Light of the Blessed Sacrament. Since she was no longer a hostage to her shame and habits, she was advancing deeper and deeper into a settled valley of sweet order, consolation, and restoration. More than a few folks at that time—unaware of her long struggles— mentioned to me, some awkwardly, that Krista's face often seemed to shimmer or take on a different light when she prayed at Adoration.

As the leaves began to change and the Year of Saint Joseph was drawing nearer to a close, Father Flum preached often on the necessity of maintaining our interior peace through prayer and the habit of virtue. It had been a dispiriting summer in America, most especially in its inner cities, where a shifting shadow seemed to push through smoke-filled night skies. The soft panic of the early summer gave way to a numbed realization that our nation's identity was changing. Consumers of cable news nightly saw a saturation of footage of moral degeneracy within the City of Man. Torched cars, violent and ungovernable riots, and looters dodging the flames of the stores they had looted filled television screens. Elderly city dwellers told reporters they kept their windows and doors locked each night as they listened to the pop-pop-pop of gunfire. They went to bed with their blinds drawn, asking for God's protection and the light of day.

The surge in what seemed a revolutionary depravity, though, wasn't restricted to inner cities. One night in the starlit valley of the Appalachian Mountains, not far from sleepy Chickamauga Lake in Chattanooga, an individual took a hacksaw to the statued head of Mary, the Queen of Peace. Her beheading came a day after the likeness of her face was set on fire in Boston. The day before, in Queens, a man with a can of black spray paint walked up to a nearly 100-year-old statue of Mary and marked her, in capital letters written vertically down her gown, *IDOL*. The inhuman spree of Marian desecration came amid the statuary beheadings of Confederate generals and even Christopher Columbus. One afternoon, in downtown Baltimore, the likeness of Columbus was pulled from its moorings and dragged into the harbor amid a loud chorus of frenzied young adults. Memorials of "white Jesus," Saint Junípero Serra, and even Abraham Lincoln were sledgehammered or removed by government authorities, who dispatched cranes to parks and downtown memorial sites, where thick harnesses were wrapped around newly spray-painted statues and lowered onto long flatbed trucks.

Something had *come into* our country. Though Father Flum never fully shared his sentiments from the pulpit, the sharper manner of his words and sermons suggested the darkening of America's soul was a consequence of the temporary denial of the sacraments and Masses. The void had given open access for the Prince of the World to broaden his malevolence and show his face in plain sight.

Accordingly, Father Flum took new measures to combat the spreading contagion of evil. Each evening, sharply at 9 P.M., unless he was called out of town for an emergency, he invoked the power of God through long-form prayers of exorcism. He knew the manner in which Holy Orders and the grace of his Office had given birth to a sacred muscularity in him. It was an underpinning of mysterious power that uniquely equipped him to square off against evil and then begin to tame it.

The waters of the age had been stirred into a foaming sludgy tide in March of 2020, and without telling a soul, he understood that his twenty-five-plus years in seminary and his priesthood had set him right for the times. From the beginning of his days of being formed in a seminary, he took extra measures to find God. He had given his priesthood to Our Lady and called on her interiorly at various points throughout the day. Few knew, but he had spent more than two decades strenuously working to strip his body and deprive it of all worldly comforts and consolations, taking on sustained fasts, self-denials, and various forms of bodily mortifications. His choice to abstain from alcohol and meat caused his frame to shrink some over the years, but he was lithe and muscled and swung an ax for hours at a time.

One morning, while watching masons setting the finishing stones at the top of the large French-styled, open-arched Marian grotto he had designed at his parish, he noticed the foreman looking down from his scaffold at a single large stone on the ground. Before the foreman was able to send his strapping laborer to wheelbarrow over the stone—which was approximately ninety pounds in weight—he watched Father Flum bend down and pick it up.

"Father," the on-site foreman warned. "Don't do it. It is too heavy for you." But at that point, the former high school athlete was already walking the stone toward the scaffolding. The masons smiled and shook their heads as he set down the stone. These were not moments to flaunt his strength; Father Flum was simply being attentive to the moment. He didn't want the masons climbing from the scaffold, and he saw that the laborer was busy with a gas-powered saw.

The strength of his prayer life, devotion to Mary, and many years of bodily renunciations had not been done in a spirit of single-minded zealotry. He simply loved the way of past saints and tried to give God all of himself so he might become a worthy victim to sustain and protect the souls of his parishioners.

Though the centerpiece of his priesthood had always been an overarching identification with the crucified Christ, the splendor of his fatherhood and care of souls came into full bloom throughout the spring, summer, and fall months, when he tempered his words like a sword during the nightly exorcism ritual. No matter where he was in the early evening—sharing a meal at a parishioner's home, visiting a sick member of the parish, or spending time with his mother an hour away—he politely excused himself and departed when his mental clock chimed for his return to Saint Michael's. He'd pull his pick-up into the lot and walk beneath a star-choked country sky toward a side door of his church.

After spending time with Christ before the Blessed Sacrament, he led the prayers of Benediction and reposition in a mostly darkened church. After a few minutes of silence, he pulled the thin chain of his small ambo lamp that seemed to act as a flare of warning. When he began the old exorcism prayers, his visage and manner seemed to be transformed. Members of "the Wings," the closely bonded group of young adults at his parish, spread out in pews on many of those nights and saw the metamorphosis. Each knew that the thunder of Father Flum's bidding to Jesus to drive out demonic infestations wasn't bombastic country-preacher theatrics; it was the baring of the core of his soul. They saw on those unforgettable nights a hatchet-wielding shepherd who seemed to be chasing down wolves.

He offered those who were there a rare glimpse of a man who seemed to have stepped into another dimension, where for ten or so minutes, he appeared to have withdrawn from the altar, his church, the town, and even the world, to engage Satan. He commanded the names of God the Father, Jesus Christ, the Mother of God, Saint Michael the Archangel, and choruses of saints and martyrs in a voice that detoured into what seemed a taunt; a goading instrument to draw down swirling demons so their necks might be snapped. As he prayed, he was picking a fight. While imploring the Heavenly court's divine protection, his usually measured voice abruptly rose and dropped, like ocean waves split by the speed and force of torpedoes. "Let God arise! Let His foes be scattered! Let those who hate Him flee from His presence. As smoke is driven away, so drive them away; like wax that melts before the fire, so the wicked shall perish at the presence of God. . . .

"I exorcize you, every unclean spirit, every power of darkness, every incursion of the infernal enemy, every diabolical legion, cohort, and faction, in the name and power of our Lord Jesus Christ! Be uprooted and put to flight from the Church of God, from souls created in the image of God and redeemed by the precious blood of the divine Lamb. . . .

"Dare no more, O cunning serpent, to deceive the human race, to persecute the Church of God, to shake the chosen of God and sift them like wheat."

Some people believe a demon visited Father Flum one night.

Depending on whom you ask, he was either attacked by an invisible presence or had tripped over a stump by his woodpile. Bizarrely, on the night in question, he had locked up the church doors and was retiring to his rectory for the evening when he went down hard onto the blacktop pavement. Although the story of his "woodpile stumble" made the rounds, it didn't make sense to those who were close to him. Father Flum was always careful with his movements and had taken the same 125-foot walk from his church to his rectory countless hundreds of times. His woodpile was twelve to fifteen feet from that path.

The morning after his fall, Father Flum arrived to celebrate Mass dragging a leg. The right side of his face was bruised, and he had a welt below his right eye. A large bandage covered a gash on his forehead. Beneath his cassock was a large wound on his right leg and shin.

At the start of Mass, he left the sacristy and noticeably winced as he genuflected to the Tabernacle. For the first time in anyone's memory, he pulled himself up by grabbing a nearby rail. As the Mass unfolded, parishioners watched Father Flum limp from place to place around the altar.

He kept the circumstances surrounding his fall private, so few discovered what happened. However, George Fritz, a close friend, rushed to the sacristy after Mass to ask what happened. Father Flum responded with a few guarded words about falling by his woodpile while walking back to his rectory the previous night.

When he said nothing more, George, who was never shy to speak what was on his mind, spoke into the silence. "Father," he said. "You know it's a sin for a priest to lie.

That woodpile has a huge light over it. It isn't anywhere near the path to the rectory."

"Your prayers requested a fight with Satan, and God allowed it. But it looks like he really kicked your ass." Father Flum smiled briefly and said nothing more. He spent the remainder of his day in his rectory.

When later his acolyte, Dave, tentatively asked him what had happened, Father Flum told him: "I'm glad you asked. It felt like I was pushed hard from behind and into the woodpile. I saw no one, and when I got up, I looked around. No one was there, no movement in any direction."

Because of the space between his path and the woodpile, Dave asked, "You were pushed all the way over there?"

Father Flum responded in an even tone: "Yes. All that way."

Much later Dave told me: "I didn't know what to say after that, so I just looked at him. It was clear to me what he was saying," Dave said. "His fall wasn't because he tripped or walked into a tree stump in the dark; he was telling me that it wasn't something natural. And I know that it wasn't natural. It was of the devil." When Dave recounted his short conversation with Father Flum, I thought of Saint John Vianney and Padre Pio, who also said they had been pushed from behind by invisible entities.

Ten or so days before his fall, Krista shared with me a dream she had had the previous night. She had seen Father Flum being pushed from behind and onto the ground by what she called a "shadow figure." Throughout the course of 2020, she told me this same "shadow figure" had entered into several of her dreams. Because of the frequency of her describing the image, I imagine I didn't pay it much mind when she told me Father Flum had been pushed into the ground by it. When she came from Mass that day and told me about Father Flum's face and body, I encouraged her to share her dream with Father Flum. When she met with him a few days later for spiritual direction, she explained her dream. As she spoke, he slowly raised up from his crouched position and listened attentively. Krista remembers him calmly responding with a single line, "The Evil One isn't happy with the Adoration happening here," he said, "and he's displeased that a soul is being taken from him."

When a parishioner discovered that Father Flum had a pull-up bar attached to the top of his bedroom closet, he asked if he made use of it. "Yes," Father Flum said. "A priest needs to be in shape if dum-dum comes." Except in prayers of exorcism, he never used the name "Satan" and often referred to the Evil One as "dum-dum."

Despite the momentary fuss over Father Flum's fall and his nightly exorcism prayers, Saint Michael's had mostly become a simple place for humble country prayer and nearly round-the-clock Adoration. As I worked to finish my manuscript, Krista began to share little stories from the time she was spending with new friends at Saint Michael's, where she often saw Father Flum hard at work on his spacious parish grounds.

There were many days after leaving Adoration that she saw Father Flum in full cassock splitting firewood alongside his young groundskeeper. One day, as they swung their axes, she eavesdropped on their conversation. Father Flum was speaking about the glories of Mary. The young man, who had been suffering from drug and alcohol abuse when Father Flum hired him around the start of COVID, later told me he had spent countless hours by the priest's side, where they mixed and poured concrete, patched holes in the church lot, shoveled up dirt to plant shrubbery and flowers, and tinkered with small maintenance projects. Mostly, though, they split firewood, where they sometimes seemed to lose their sense of time and swung their axes for hours.

"Father Flum pulled me out of a deep pit," the young man said. "He did it by keeping a close eye and getting his hands dirty with me. As we worked, he spoke to me about spiritual things, of God's natural law, and the *Catechism*. He loved to talk about the saints. He spoke to me about the consequences of sin and certain philosophies on how we can know an act is sinful.

"He told me once he didn't eat meat so he could purposefully malnourish his body. He explained it was the way of the anchorites, who knew eating meat could inflame their passions. In a way, he had become my father and Saint Michael's had become like a kind of old Boystown for me, with a holy priest who was helping me turn things around."

One afternoon, Krista drove home from a Holy Hour and saw Father Flum in his cassock dragging a large piece of metal to his truck from a sheet-metal yard. Another day, she saw him running bases in a softball game with the Wings. A young woman who had been playing that day later poured out her soul to Father Flum in confession. She had invited an evil into her life. After she told him the full story of the bleak circumstances, he encouraged daily Mass, frequent Holy Hours, and daily recitation of the Rosary. As she followed the path he had laid out, she felt her heart begin to grow and the evil fragment. At this writing, she is discerning religious life. "When I told him that I wanted to enter a religious community, he said, 'If you are serious—go, and never once look back.' He had that blazing look in his eye. He gave me every single thing he had to help me then. He led me to this place."

Meanwhile, while Father Flum began to direct the young woman spiritually, he was directing another member of the Wings, a young man raised in a family with little faith. Krista told me she had seen him frequently pull into the parish parking lot for Adoration at various points of the day. Often, the two found themselves alone together in Adoration, where Krista had taken to including him in her prayers. Because they never encountered one another outside of the church, they had never met. One evening, with her eyes closed and praying the Rosary, she saw an image of Mary standing before five or six priests. One of them was that young man, who was now wearing a collar. Krista extemporaneously left her pew and approached him, "I'm sorry for interrupting," she whispered. "But I feel like Mary wants you to become a priest."

Krista didn't know then that Father Flum had already been in the process of helping him discern the priesthood. At this writing, the young man is a seminarian in the Archdiocese of Washington.

One cool day in October, Krista shared with me while getting ready for bed the temptation to drink in secret had come back. She explained that the impulse suddenly rose in her a few times a day. Although her eyes carried the weight of the struggle, I didn't see the shadows behind them, and our bedroom ceiling didn't feel like it was collapsing.

"I promise you I haven't drunk," she said. "I've rejected it."

"I know you have," I assured her. "I'm not concerned about that."

We were sitting on the edge of the bed. I asked her to try to explain the manner in which the urge came on. She tried her best to walk me through how the impulse came earlier in the day.

"Everything was fine. I was folding clothes, and it just came," she said. "I wasn't thinking about anything that would have led to the thought. There wasn't any tension, and all of a sudden, I heard the voice from the past."

"Does it come on as strong as it used to?" I asked.

"Yes. It's the voice of my shame," Krista said calmly. "It's the voice of the devil. I know it because the voice is always telling me I can get away with it. That I can control it and do it just once. He brings me into the past where the shame is, where I always gave in.

"But every time, I've asked Mary to take it. And she has, and it goes away."

"Man, Krista," I responded from my gut. "I'm proud of you. But none of it surprises me. The fact that you're openly sharing all this is God's grace at work."

"Kevin, the urges feel different. They don't happen at Mass or when I'm praying, and everything is fine on the drives to and from Saint Michael's," she said. "Back at home, everything feels right. I'm at peace. I feel light. Then, a thought to drink comes on out of nowhere. Sometimes it's very strong ... but even then, I feel a strength I didn't have in the past."

I thought then, for the first time, that her demon of shame was pushing up against something to which it was unaccustomed. It was wheedling a soul in the process of being sanctified by God. Krista's daily reception of the Eucharist, regular confessions, and long hours in front of the Blessed Sacrament were transforming her. Father Flum told her long ago the simple act of regularly adoring Jesus at the Holy Hour would begin to give birth to a languorous peace, where rays of love would warm and fully cure her. He told her nothing on earth would be more medicinal for her soul than the act of simply keeping Him company at Adoration and gazing upon His Face in the monstrance.

He explained to her Jesus' mannerly way: As she presented herself before the Blessed Sacrament, He would begin to draw her into friendship. In time, as she expanded her time and visits with Him, Jesus would inflame in her heart a desire to please Him and to have no will but His. Within the interplay of love, she would slowly begin to feel herself detaching from worldly concerns and trials and feel herself becoming enfolded into the tender blaze of His love. As the depth of love in His Sacred Heart became revealed, he explained the manner in which Jesus would enter into her wounds: As she contemplated His earthly life and embracing care for her, He would begin to reveal the hidden obstacles and sins that barred a more intimate friendship with Him. In that self-awareness and identification of the barriers, He would gently pour into her soul mysterious movements of unnoticed grace, insights, and consolations to set in motion the interior disposition that would lead to her total conversion.

When, a few days later in his office, I told Father Flum about our conversation and the unwelcome sword of Damocles, he smiled peacefully behind his beard. The Evil One, he said with nonchalance, hated that Krista was drawing close to Christ. His attempts to rake lies of unworthiness and shame into her conscience were old hat. "The Evil One hates that he's losing Krista," he said. "As long as she continues on her path of opening herself to God at Mass and Adoration, she'll be fine."

Then, abruptly, he turned his attention to me. He said Krista's willingness to expose her urge to drink was a marvelous gesture of spousal vulnerability and love. He reminded me of what I already knew: Krista was in a different place; Jesus had placed into her soul cascades of spiritual tools to beat back her tempters.

"I want to let you know something that is happening now. As Krista is healing, for the first time, she can see you. Maybe for the first time in your marriage, she is asking for your strength. She is pleading with you to be strong for her. For all the right reasons, Krista is afraid, and she is asking you to help and protect her." His words were illuminative. Although they were simple and straight-forward, they seemed to have been peeled from scrolls discovered in a Palestine cave. It had never occurred to me that her vulnerability was also a request for me to help see her through the diabolic pokes that were coming her way.

Father Flum smiled widely, the assuring look of con-fidence a manager gives his closer when handing him the baseball in a late-inning crisis. "For the first time, she wants you to lead her through this," he said. "Make sure you're staying very close to God as well, so He can lead you to do it as He wills."

He reached into his well-stocked bookshelf and pulled out a pair of old books on the life of Saint Joseph. "These two are good," he said. "I want you to read them both. Saint Joseph will help you now." He was telling me to become Krista's Saint Joseph.

Early one morning, three weeks later, at around 3:30 A.M., as All Hallow's Eve was giving way to All Saint's Day, Krista experienced something unexplainable.

She had joined her friend Mary Pastore for Adoration at Sacred Heart parish in La Plata, Maryland. In his candle-lit church, Father Larry Swink, a pastor and long-time friend of mine, had just led the Rosary for fifteen or so bleary-eyed souls. Father Swink had twice led prayers of deliver-ance over Krista in two Unbound sessions. After the first session, he told me, "Kevin, Krista was manifesting. I can only think of one or two other times when things became more intense during exorcism prayers."

Ten or so minutes after the Rosary, with her eyes closed and kneeling on the floor, Krista remembers feeling the visceral presence of Our Lady. Never in her life had she experienced anything like it.

These are Krista's words of the memory:

Mary stood before me. My eyes were closed, but I saw her standing before me, maternal and loving. She seemed there, not in imagination, but there concretely.

She clearly began to motion for me to follow her. So, I did. We began to walk, as if she were leading me somewhere. I heard her voice within me saying that she would protect me. After a while, Mary stopped, then she encouraged me to kneel. When I looked up, I saw Jesus at the altar.

I looked at Mary, and she looked at me with a smile—and she nodded. She told me to give it to Him.

I knew what she meant; I had to release everything—the secret drinking, the fears to live without it, all the shame. She wanted me to release all the things I was still holding onto. She asked me to surrender it all to her Son.

I began to cry because I didn't want to do it. I was scared to live without it. I kept telling her in pleading tears, "I can't do it, I can't do it." Finally, she looked at me and gently said that she wouldn't leave my side. Then, she said her Son wanted it, and to give it to Him. She said He was already helping me, that I was already on my way.

That's the moment I gave it all up, placing it on the altar, and He took it away.

Three years later, as of this writing, everything has changed. Krista has been liberated.

She texted Father Flum a few hours later at daybreak and told him that something extraordinary had happened the previous night. He texted her right back and asked for her to see him right after Mass.

Directly following the celebration of the All Saints' Day Mass, he did something he had never previously done. He poked his head out of the sacristy door and motioned her in from her customary pew in front of the statue of Our Lady. After entering, Krista saw him right there, on the other side of the door. She told him that Mary had visited her. She told him of her surrender. As she shed tears, Father Flum smiled like a father regarding his daughter on her wedding day. She had crossed over, he knew. After having spent countless hours with Mary in meditative prayer—Our Lady knew Krista's soul had been tilled and reshaped. It was time for Krista finally to surrender herself to her Son.

After Krista finished her story, Father Flum did something else he had never done. He embraced her tightly for a long time. When they parted, she saw that his eyes were glistening. He couldn't speak. So he smiled warmly at his spiritual daughter, slowly nodded his head, and walked away.

AFTERWORD

On a blue-sky June morning eight months later, Krista
was praying at Adoration when a friend of hers, Chris
Bowman, approached her after leaving the confessional.
"Father Flum would like to talk to you," she whispered
into her ear.

As Krista walked to the rear of the church, she saw him
sitting on a wooden pew in the cry room.

She opened the door and sat beside him. He smiled
warmly at her through his wild beard, and Krista felt
silence cover the room. The world was about to change.

"Krista, you know my heart. I want to tell you something that will be public in a few days," he said. He looked
piercingly into her eyes and spoke gently. "For a long time,
my heart has desired to be only in prayer. God has called
me to solitude. I am going to leave soon to begin the life
of a hermit. God has called me to the eremitical life for a
long while now ... and I know it's time for me to go."

Krista felt a soft tremor cover her as sunlight poured
through the window beside him. She turned from facing him and looked toward the altar and golden-sunburst
monstrance, where her eyes clung to the Host as if they
were the fingertips of the hemorrhaging woman. As an
inner volcano of emotions rose in her, Father Flum let
silence permeate the space and kept his gaze on my broken flower's wilted face. I imagine his heart was struck by
Krista's extemporaneous pivot to Jesus in the Blessed Sacrament. It had been the anchorage point to which he had

so often led the past few years. It was a rare day that she didn't spend an hour or two, or more, at her spot between the "collapsing love" of the hidden Jesus in the Host and the statue of what had become her favorite image of Our Lady. She had knelt there so often that occasionally she had seen herself there in dreams.

As she worked to pull her emotions together, she said something that surprised Father Flum. "Well, Monsignor Esseff told me this would happen one day," she said with teary eyes and a small smile. "He knew you would be leaving to become a hermit, so I can't say I'm caught completely off-guard."

"He said that to you?" Father Flum asked.

"Yes," she said, turning back to face him. "So, in a way, I knew. How much longer will you be around?"

"I leave in about three weeks," he said softly. He looked into her glazed eyes. "Krista, do you understand that you are a new creation, that you're in a different place? Jesus and Our Lady have brought you to a new life, and you are resting in their love for you now."

Krista felt the burning in her eyes again. But like a trembling daughter hoping to stay brave before the sight of her father, she fought her tears and looked into his face.

"You and your family have never been in a better place. Krista, keep on your path," he said. "You've discovered the most important thing—you know God's love for you. Keep going deeper and deeper into that love—because now He needs you to bring His love to others. You are His beloved daughter, and He is well pleased with you, Krista."

She turned back to the Sacred Host, where her eyes filled again. She couldn't speak.

"Krista, don't ever look back," Father Flum said. "Everything is going to be fine from here on out."

The room fell as silent as Atlantis on the bottom of the sea.

After a while, Krista said in a quivering voice: "If God led you to this, then I'm happy. Thank you, Father Flum, for everything." She wanted to say more, but her emotions prevented it. Krista felt a strange mingling of brokenheartedness and peacefulness rise in her. It was a heart brimming over with love. She knew Father Flum was disappearing to become Beloved John, where he would spend the remainder of his life resting his head against Jesus' heart.

Krista rose on wobbly legs, opened the door, and walked to the parking lot. She pulled her car onto the country lanes and began to cry. A guillotine had just split her soul into two pieces. Already she knew one part of her would hold memories of the man who saved her, and the other would forever mourn. When Krista turned left onto Croom Road, she was weeping like a mother who had just lost her son in war.

On June 29, 2021, the play-by-play of the Orioles-Astros game was playing in the background when Father Flum joined us for another of Krista's steaming pots of shrimp Fra Diavolo. When we sat down around the patio table in our backyard, the sun was slowly moving below the tall trees in our back field. The tangy-sweet aroma of Krista's homemade sauce merged with the hum of crickets, frogs, birds, and the soft voice-over of baseball that hung in the air like the incense of a lazy summer routine. Nothing, of course, seemed normal. In a few days, we would never see Father Flum again on this side of eternity.

I sat in the chair facing the Marian grotto that muscle memory told me would soon be bathed in light. Krista sat across the table from Father Flum. I remember noticing that night that his beard had whitened some and grown unrulier. He had grown out his beard early in his priesthood to "appear unattractive" to women when a pair of undesired romantic advances came his way. He had on the faded cassock that was as much a part of him as wings are to cherubim. He glowed that evening and was as relaxed as I had ever seen him. Indeed, it seemed parts of him were already breaking off, as if he were gradually vanishing from the natural world, in the fashion of Shoeless Joe Jackson when he stepped into the outfield cornfield in *Field of Dreams*.

Father Flum blessed the meal, and we began to eat. I remember stealing sidelong glances at Krista as Father Flum told us about the flurry of activity at Saint Michael's as he prepared his parish for the incoming pastor. He was in the midst of repaving Saint Michael's parking lot and ridding himself of all of his possessions. As he leisurely spoke of the rush of activity, I kept looking out of the corner of my eye at Krista in what started to feel like uncontrollable twitches. Over and over, though, my looks revealed the same thing—her face was as bright and peaceful as Father Flum's, as if he had permitted her entrance into the languid movements of his soul. A surreal peace covered everything—and I suddenly felt like I was eavesdropping on the sacred undercurrents of the symbiosis of a spiritual father with his spiritual daughter.

As the sky darkened and the grotto brightened, Krista and I began for the first time to ask him about his new life. Although he spoke in a relaxed manner about his call to enter perhaps the world's rarest vocation, we could see in the softness of his gaze that he was already partly there. For so many years, endless acres of his soul had felt trapped. Although he was a hardworking pastor who loved to serve his flock, he had hungered for a long time for total solitude with God and to offer himself as a victim through unending prayer, penances, and mortifications.

"I know it's an unusual calling, but it is real," he said, with a humble smile. "For many years, even in seminary, there was an ever-deepening desire for ongoing contemplative prayer, where 'God alone' is the only desire.

"Oftentimes, the eremitic life was seen, by those not familiar with it, as a vacation—where one would build a little hut and stir his soup and watch the birds and sunrise from his wooden porch. But no. The hermit's life is 'God alone.' It is to live the crucified life of Christ; it is living His Passion in a way the active priest cannot."

Only a few souls knew his hermitage's location. He politely requested that no one visit and asked those who discovered his location to respect the solitariness of his vocation. We heard from a reliable source that Father Flum's entire "house" would be, in essence, a rustic hermitage no larger than a child's bedroom. His home, simply, was a small cell for him to adore Christ. The peal of monastery bells that would mark his hours and days of union with God could be heard—but just barely—through a thicket of tens of thousands of trees on the grounds of a cloistered Order of nuns.

His cell would lack heat, plumbing, and electricity. A rain catcher, we heard from a friend of his, would capture his drinking water. A small patch of grass by his cell would allow him to grow a small garden that would provide his sustenance. We couldn't have known, though, if all we learned was factual because he was tight-lipped about all details, holding them like sacred secrets.

Father Flum did, though, share with Krista and me a few blurry images and scraps of information of his call within a call to offer his life to God as a poured chalice. I imagined him kneeling on a winter night, attempting an all-night vigil as snow fell—then curling his body for sleep before the candle lighting his monstrance.

He spoke with solemnity of the hermit's debt. "He pursues his vocation because God is beckoning him into the wilderness of a relationship solely with Him. The distinctive mark of a consecrated hermit is separation from everyone else and giving himself entirely to God," he said. "The Church needs her members truly to live their vocation. If the hand decides to be an ear, the body loses something. The Church is impoverished; so, in a real way, the austere life of a hermit is a type of service to the Church. It's unusual, but for a great while I have felt called to live it."

He went on to describe a typical day of the hermit, which began in moonlight, usually between 3 and 4 A.M., when he rose from sleep and knelt for Prime. The first of his Liturgy of the Hours is much fuller, richer, and longer than the one that almost all other clergy pray. The hermit is given more Psalms and nocturns to pray and contemplate. He said that his first office, if prayed with love, would unfold in no less than an hour. Prayer, he said, would soon permeate each of his waking hours and perhaps even begin to filter into his dreams as a type of half-aware doxology.

His prayer would sanctify time itself.

"The hermit lives as a sign and witness to priests that God is due everything—wholly and completely—no Redskins games, no entertainment, etc.; we need to live entirely for souls, and souls alone. I'm going to be the best that I can. I'm just a novice, though. One doesn't just *become* a hermit ... like Scripture says: 'He set his face like flint.' The hermit knows his task, and his task is to go to the Cross."

I asked him in a moment of rudeness if he expected to be attacked, in the manner of Saint Anthony of the Desert, by Satan. He looked at me without emotion, then looked at Krista. He said plainly that a hermit in the state of grace should anticipate demonic assailants. The very nature of his vocation to crucify his life with Christ, he said, invited war with Satan. He broke the ice with a small story.

"There is a description from a Church Father that there was a city caught up in sin—but it was left alone by demons, who instead attacked the monastery outside the city gates," he said. "The demons knew they had to work harder to destroy the city by harassing and destroying the prayers of the monks who had offered themselves for that city."

He continued: "There is full confidence in God, but there is also some trepidation with that realm. The Evil One's intellect is more powerful than mine, but God's grace is more powerful," he said. "If I'm not headstrong and remember fighting off demons doesn't depend on me—there is a confidence [when Satan comes].... Of course, there is a proper reverential fear of entities working to pull me away from God, but I also know what Teresa of Ávila eventually said to Satan: 'Oh, it's just you.'

"There is a certain peace that comes from acknowledging the methods and work of the demon. People are afraid of the Evil One, but we must understand who he is, and what he is—and, most importantly, that he has been defeated. He is a huckster, a magician. He tries to trick us into believing he is more dangerous than he is. He is a liar. All his power is derived from how God has created him. When we live in the grace of the Lord, though, the demon knows he is coming up against both me and the Lord."

Shaken and disquieted, Krista asked the priest she loved if Satan frightened him. He stayed quiet for a few seconds in gathering his thoughts. Perhaps wanting to placate his spiritual daughter's visible concern for him, he answered sanguinely.

"Well, Krista—dealing with the demon might be like going to your first fight and bringing along your older brother—so, you're scared, but not that scared," he said, assuring her with a wide smile. "You feel, in a way, very protected. And, there is God, there is Mary, my guardian angel, and Saint Michael whom I'm taking with me." He then shared with Krista stories of hermits down the ages—Saint Dominic Loricatus, Pope Celestine V, Saint Charbel, and others—who warded off spiritual attacks through unceasing devotion, severe penances, and by rigorously committing to their mortified life for souls.

Word had spread at Saint Michael's that he was offering his life for the recovery of the priesthood. He had been deeply troubled and saddened by the Church's response to the pandemic. Ever the journalist, I asked if the parish rumor was factual. He answered diplomatically: "If the priest is truly going to imitate Christ, he is going to live a penitential life. He will live a life of prayer and penance. The hermit is a reminder to the priest that this life is supposed to be a penance. It's living the vocation in its fullness. . . . Because of his duties, the diocesan priest isn't able to live this form of penitential life—the hermit can live it, though—even beyond what Saint John Vianney did as far as penitential life. The hermit is to imitate Christ even more intensely. Life becomes *God alone.*"

Every now and then, as Father Flum revealed in words the secret heart of the hermit, Krista and I looked at each other. We knew we were listening to the words of a man who desired to become an undiscussed saint. His voice in a few days would become an endless flow of praise to God. His heart, hands, intellect, comfort, his entire life would soon be handed over to the Eternal Father. We smiled at each other, even though we knew he would soon become a ghost.

It was late when we walked Father Flum to his silver high-mileage pick-up truck with the faded MARY-land bumper sticker. I shook his hand and said a few clumsy well-wishes and thank-yous. Krista embraced him and said loving words I couldn't hear. His truck was parked in the same spot as five years earlier, when he drove out for dinner and was turned away by a woman who no longer was.

I held Krista as we watched him pull out of our driveway for the last time. As his taillights disappeared past a treeline on Isabella Court, we stayed quiet for a while. She remembers me telling her that we were going to be okay. I believed it that night, and I believe it, far more, these three years later.

As we stood alone under the moon, it seemed we had reached the top of some sort of mountain. It was time to begin to walk down and to see the other side.

Inside, I heard excited voices from the television. The Orioles had exploded for a five-run, late-inning rally against the best team in baseball. I watched for a minute, then turned it off. I needed Krista. And she needed me.

ACKNOWLEDGMENTS

I am especially grateful to Jennifer Brinker, Constance Hull, Rob Marco, and Bill Quinn, who, one by one, encouraged me to see that the book I had written was not the one I thought. Your wisdom and insights are like jewels. Justin McClain, thank you for stepping in to mind my grammatical p's and q's. I'd like to note my great fortune to work again with the editorial team at Ignatius Press.

I am indebted to Father Larry Swink, Father Dan Leary, and Monsignor John Esseff for their friendships and spiritual aid.

Gabrielle, Sean, and Shannon, there is no prouder dad.

On the other side, I hope to find Father Martin Flum and thank him for diving to the bottom for the pearl.

And to my wounded healer, whom I love—thanks for pushing me to "write through". *The Hermit*'s done. It's your turn, my brave-hearted Krista. I even picked out a title: *The Other Side of the Mountain*.

Now, write.